Guitar
Technique

Bridges®
A Comprehensive Guitar Series

FREDERICK HARRIS MUSIC

Bridges®
A Comprehensive Guitar Series

The *Guitar Series* was originally published in 1989 to international acclaim. The second edition (1997) and third edition (2004) built on that strong foundation and the present fourth edition has been substantially updated and refined to meet the demands of modern teaching and learning.

Some of the notable new features of this edition are the addition of guitar masterpieces by the most beloved guitar composers including Agustín Barrios, Heitor Villa-Lobos, and Leo Brouwer; a substantial reduction in the amount of fingering given, leaving teachers more flexibility and a clearer score from which to work; and an improved balance of style choices for repertoire and studies in all levels. This edition aims to provide students with a clear, well-paced route for their musical development; to nurture the technique necessary to successfully meet those developmental challenges; and to expose students to the full range of the instrument's repertoire.

The well-rounded guitarist will have an understanding of the instrument's history, as well as practical experience with a wide range of repertoire from all historical periods and styles. Guided by this principle, the series editors have drawn on more than 500 years' worth of guitar and lute music. Each book features compositions from the Renaissance to the present day; by learning music from each style period, students will gain a comprehensive overview of the evolution of musical styles. The studies/etudes have been chosen for building technique and musicality specifically relevant to the repertoire of each level. Technical and conceptual challenges are progressively introduced from one book to the next to ensure the steady development of musical skills.

The guitar student who works carefully through this series under the guidance of a good teacher will gain not only technical proficiency, but also artistic maturity and a broad overview of the instrument's repertoire. Because the chosen repertoire and studies/etudes at any given level fall within a carefully sequenced range of technical and musical difficulty, from the late-elementary (Preparatory–1) to late-intermediate and early advanced levels (Levels 7–8), students can be assured that their learning path will be well rounded and complete.

A Note on Editing and Performance

A systematic and thorough approach to fingering is fundamental to a student's success in learning to play the classical guitar. The fingerings in this series have been designed in accordance with the latest pedagogical principles and to ensure natural playability and musical integrity. The use of fingering indications throughout the nine *Repertoire and Studies* books and the *Guitar Technique* book is intended to provide a logical framework for the development of a musically fluent and flexible guitar technique without the clutter of redundant markings. Students are encouraged to know both the right- and left-hand fingering for the entire piece and to mark fingerings in the score in consultation with their teachers where none are suggested.

Faithfulness to the composers' intentions, as reflected in the source materials, has guided the editors' decisions concerning the inclusion of dynamic markings. It should be noted that the absence of dynamic markings in the scores does not imply that the music should be performed without dynamic contrast, only that no markings were given in the source material.

Metronome markings for the repertoire and studies suggest tempos within accepted stylistic ranges and technical considerations. A tempo range is given to accommodate individual interpretations. In the interest of personal creativity, teachers and students may wish to alter the given dynamic indications and metronome markings, or to employ alternate fingerings.

For assessment requirements of The Royal Conservatory and the Music Development Program, please refer to the *Guitar Syllabus*, 2011 Edition.

Robert Hamilton　　*Dr. Jeffrey McFadden*

Contents

Introduction

Part 1: Technical Requirements by Level

Part 1 contains technical requirements for guitar examinations of The Royal Conservatory. Performance objectives and suggested practice methods of each technical component are given below. In preparing for the technical portion of a guitar examination, students should consult the *Guitar Syllabus, 2011 Edition,* in conjunction with *Guitar Technique.*

Diatonic and Chromatic Scales

Objective: In preparing diatonic and chromatic scales, strive for consistent volume and articulation, steadiness of tempo, perfect *legato* articulation, and a consistent and refined tone.

Suggested practice method: Begin by playing slowly with a metronome and gradually increase the tempo, listening carefully for the maintenance of control, clarity, evenness, and good tone. Practice scales in both rest stroke and free stroke, using the finger combinations and accent patterns listed on p. 5. Finish the diatonic scales with the appropriate chord or cadence.

Tremolando Scales

Objective: Tremolando (repeated-note) scales may be played to develop right-hand speed and dexterity. Strive for consistent volume and articulation, steadiness of tempo, perfect *legato* articulation, and a consistent and refined tone.

Suggested practice method: Prepare tremolando scales in the same manner as diatonic and chromatic scales, giving special attention to right-hand articulation. Listen carefully for clarity of accents and consistency of volume in all finger combinations.

Slur Scales

Objective: In preparing slur scales, strive for rhythmic accuracy and a consistent volume between plucked and slurred notes.

Suggested practice method: Pay special attention to left-hand finger trajectory. Practice smaller segments of the scale, devoting an appropriate degree of extra time to strengthen weaker-finger combinations (for example, 3–4 pull-offs and hammer-ons). Listen carefully for the balance between plucked and slurred notes. Practice with a metronome and gradually increase the speed.

Scales in 3rds and 6ths

Objective: Strive for simultaneity of note pairs, balance of volume, and perfect *legato* articulation.

Suggested practice method: To achieve right-hand balance and simultaneity, practice scales in a tremolando format, repeating each dyad three or four times. Practice the left hand separately, emphasizing finger preparation to achieve a seamless quality.

Arpeggio Patterns

Objective: Strive for a perfect note-to-note clarity in rhythm, volume, and tone. Listen for precision in the timing of chord changes.

Suggested practice method: Practice with a metronome, starting at a tempo that facilitates control and clarity. Gradually increase the tempo while maintaining right-hand stability, as well as regulated finger-speed and trajectory. Most of the arpeggios have been selected from *120 Arpeggios,* op. 1 by Mauro Giuliani.

Part 2: Technique Supplement

Part 2 offers a variety of fingerings, rhythms, and supplementary exercises used by professional guitarists to vary their daily practice routine. Incorporate these supplementary components as needed, to strengthen rhythmic control, build speed, and improve flexibility in your guitar technique.

Accent and Fingering Patterns

The *im* combination may be executed as either *i–m* or *m–i*
The *ia* combination may be executed as either *i–a* or *a–i*
The *ma* combination may be executed as either *m–a* or *a–m*

Diatonic and Chromatic Scales

Two-finger combinations—quarter-note accents
(Preparatory–Level 2)

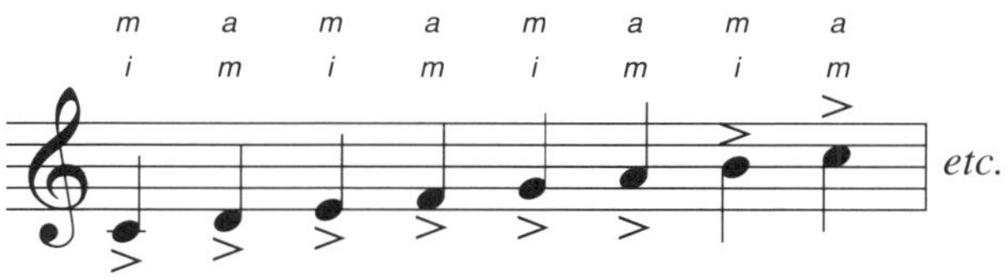

Two-finger combinations—eighth-note accents
(Levels 3–4)

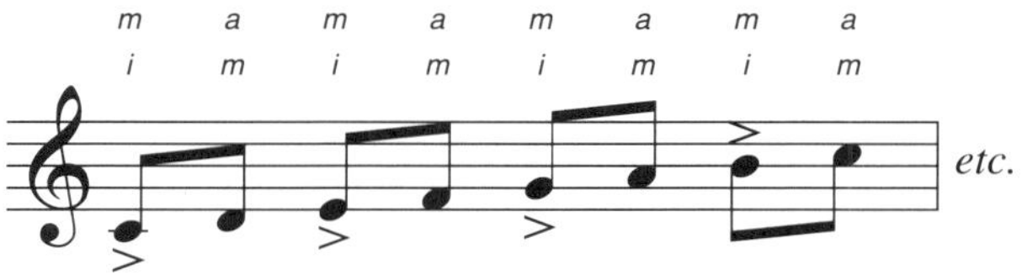

Two-finger combinations—triplet accents
(Levels 4–ARCT)

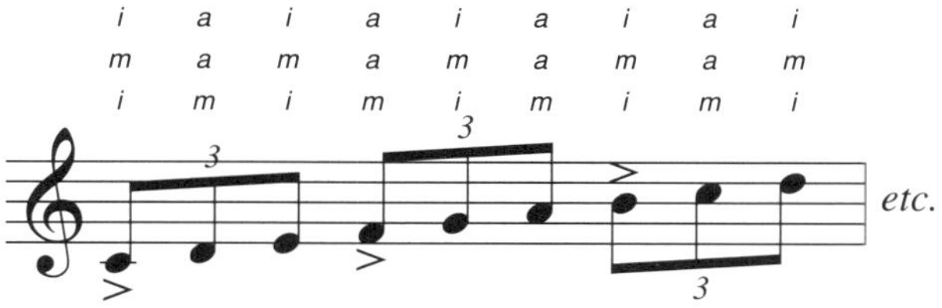

Two-finger combinations—sixteenth-note accents
(Levels 5–ARCT)

Tremolando Scales

Two-finger combinations—eighth-note accents
(Preparatory–Level 3)

Two-finger combinations—triplets
(Levels 5–ARCT)

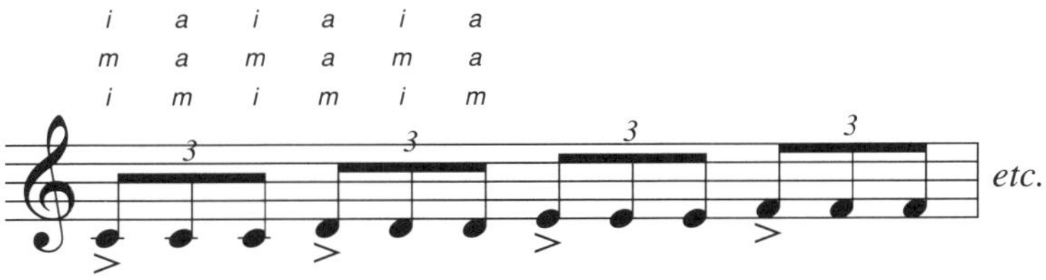

Two-finger combinations—quadruplets
(Levels 4–ARCT)

Part 1: Technical Requirements by Level

Preparatory Level

Diatonic Scales

Play the following scales, in both rest stroke and free stroke, at or beyond the tempo given in the chart. Follow the left-hand fingering precisely and finish each scale with the given chord. Play each scale with the note values and the right-hand fingering listed in the chart. See "Accent and Fingering Patterns" on p. 5.

Keys	Tempo	Note Values	RH Fingering
C, G major A, E minor (harmonic and melodic)	♩ = 80	♩	*im* or *mi* *ma* or *am*

C Major (1 octave)

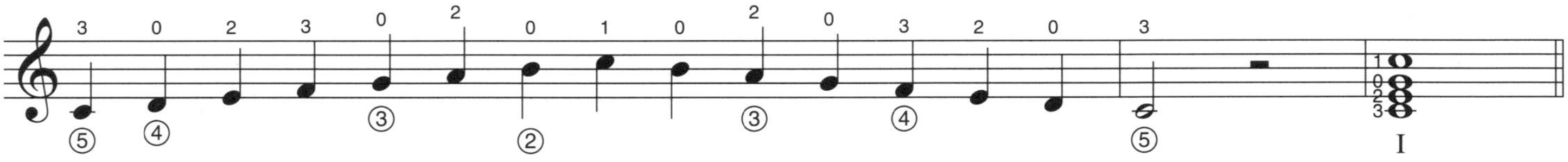

A Minor Harmonic (1 octave)

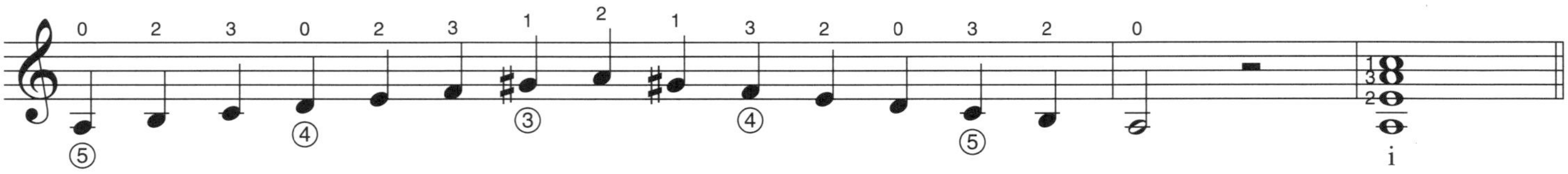

A Minor Melodic (1 octave)

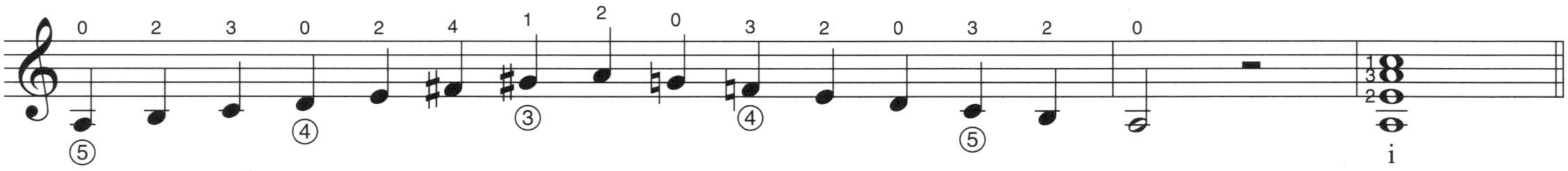

G Major (1 octave)

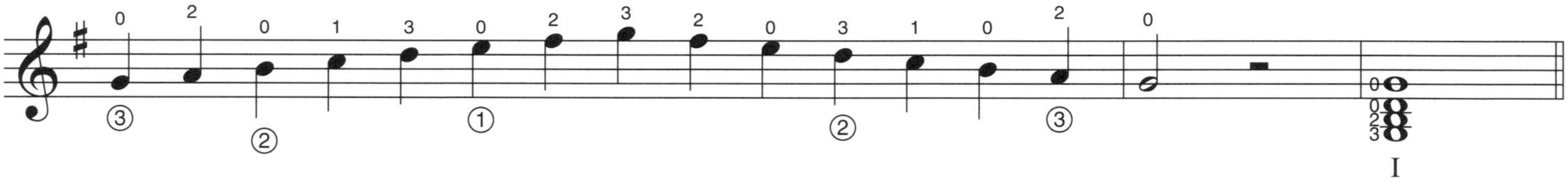

E Minor Harmonic (1 octave)

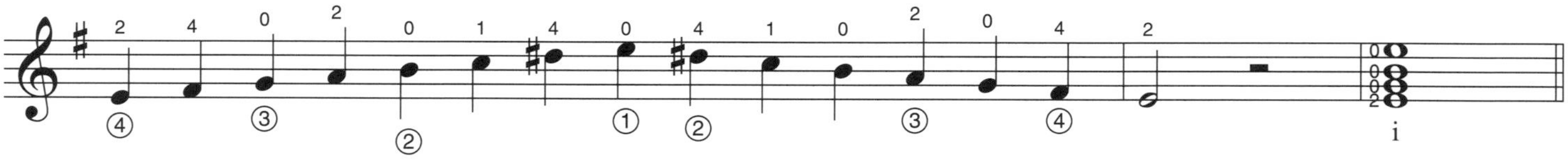

E Minor Melodic (1 octave)

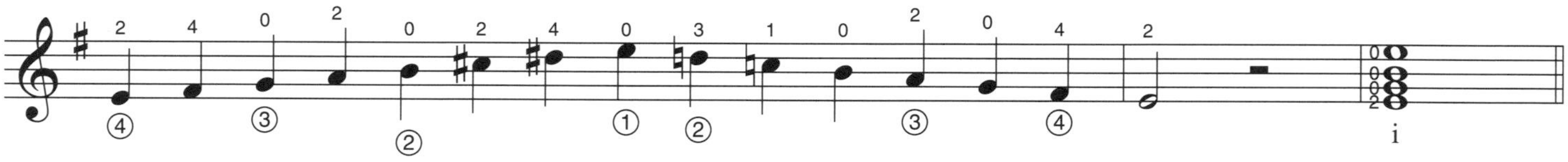

Tremolando Scales

Play all the single-note diatonic scales illustrated above in tremolando, with both rest stroke and free stroke, at or beyond the tempo given in the chart. Follow the left-hand fingering precisely and finish each scale with the given chord. Play each scale with the note values and the right-hand fingering listed in the chart. See "Accent and Fingering Patterns" on p. 5.

Keys	Tempo	Note Values	RH Fingering
C, G major A, E minor (harmonic and melodic)	♩ = 56	♫♫	*im* or *mi* *ma* or *am*

Arpeggio Patterns

Play the following arpeggio patterns at or beyond the given tempo. Use the given fingering and observe the repeat signs.

1. *p–m–i* triplet pattern

♩ = 69

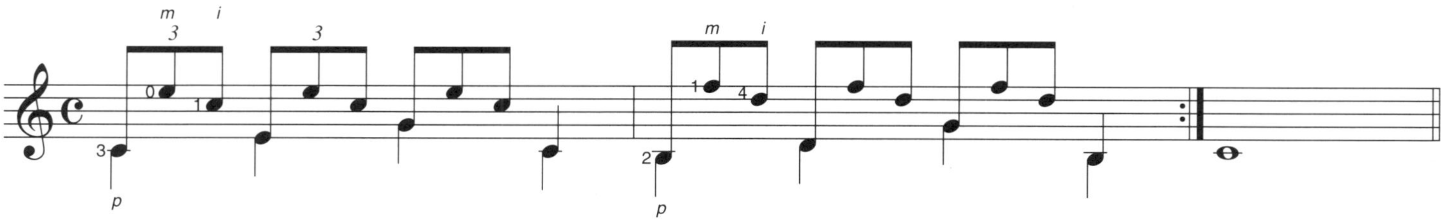

2. *p–i–m* triplet pattern

♩ = 69

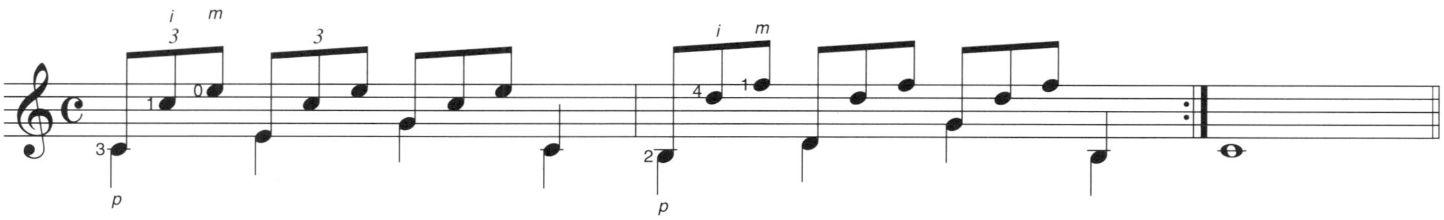

3. *p–a–i* triplet pattern

♩ = 69

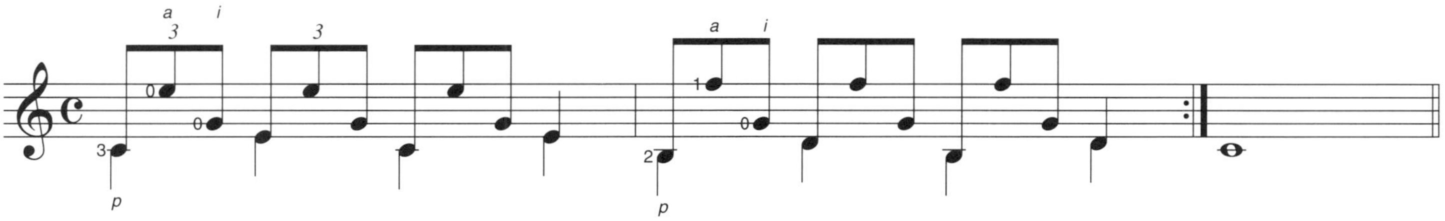

4. *p–i–a* triplet pattern

♩ = 69

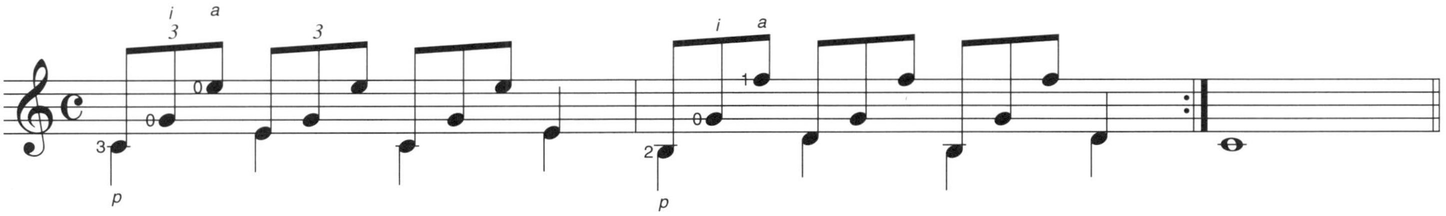

Level 1

Diatonic and Chromatic Scales

Play the following scales, in both rest stroke and free stroke, at or beyond the tempo given in the chart. Follow the left-hand fingering precisely and finish each diatonic scale with the given cadence. Play each scale with the note values and the right-hand fingering listed in the chart. See "Accent and Fingering Patterns" on p. 5.

	Keys	Tempo	Note Values	RH Fingering
Diatonic	G, D, F major E, B, D minor (harmonic and melodic)	♩ = 100	♩	*im* or *mi* *ma* or *am*
Chromatic	Beginning on D			

Diatonic Scales

G Major (2 octaves)

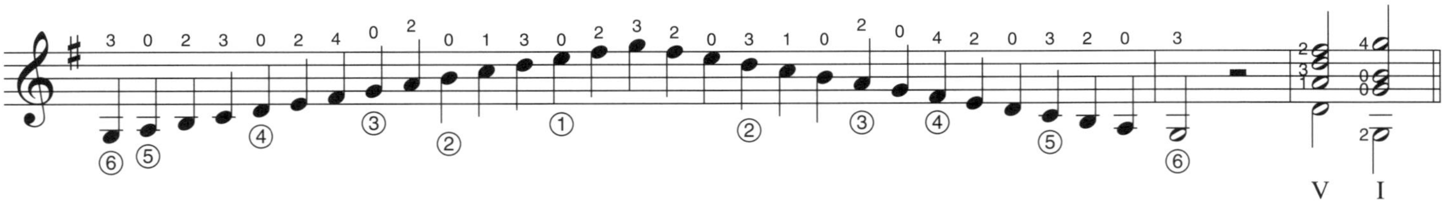

E Minor Harmonic (2 octaves)

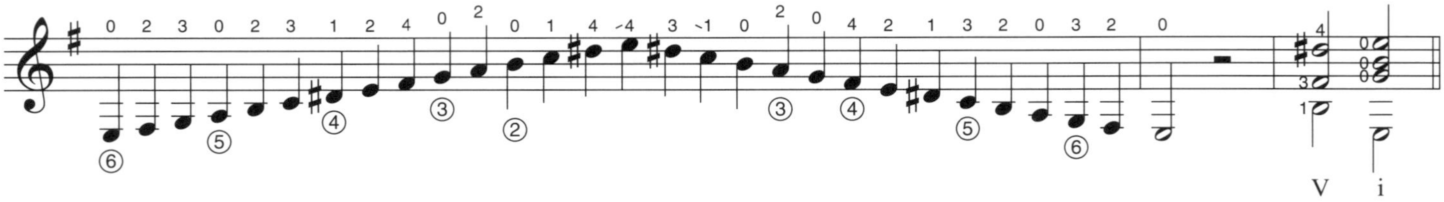

E Minor Melodic (2 octaves)

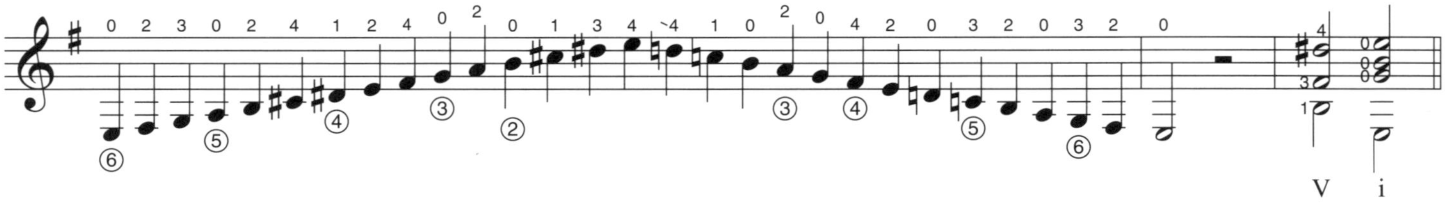

D Major (1 octave)

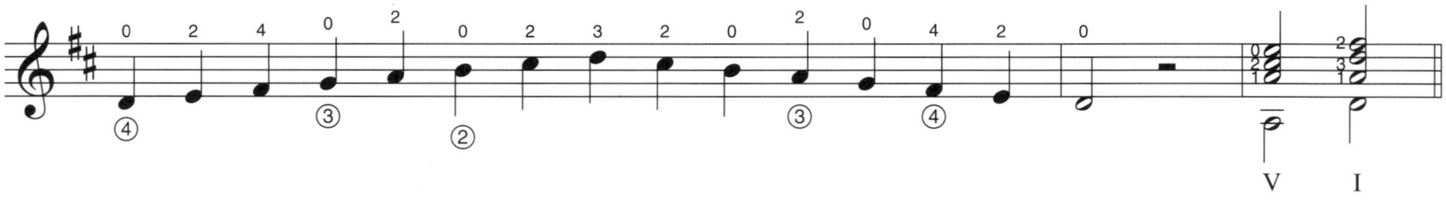

B Minor Harmonic (1 octave)

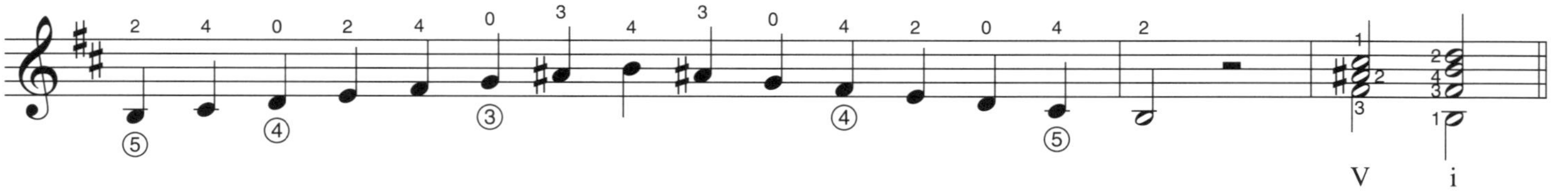

B Minor Melodic (1 octave)

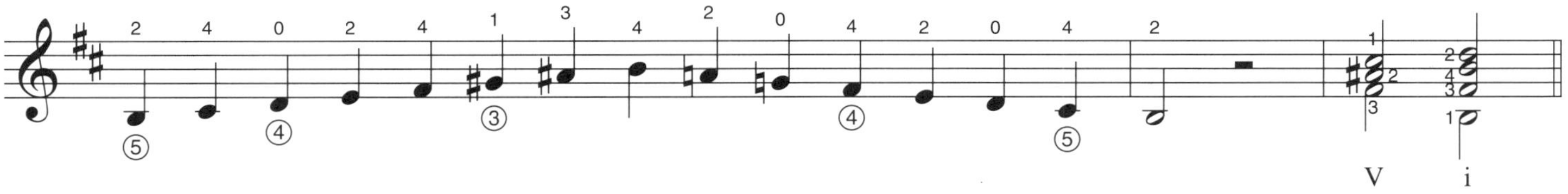

F Major (1 octave)

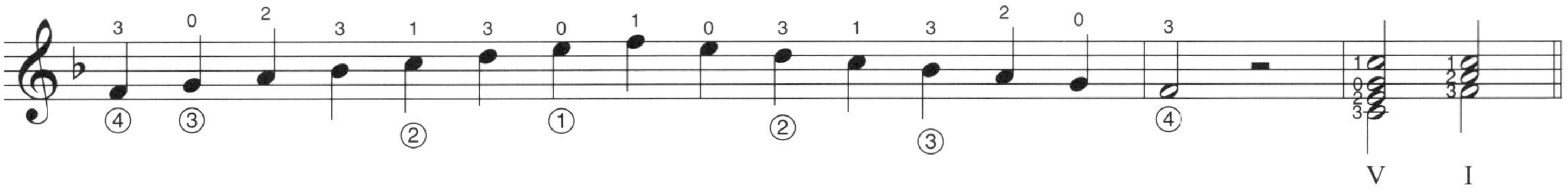

D Minor Harmonic (1 octave)

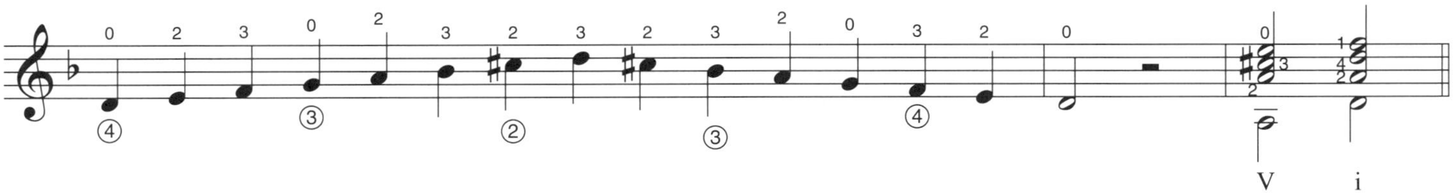

D Minor Melodic (1 octave)

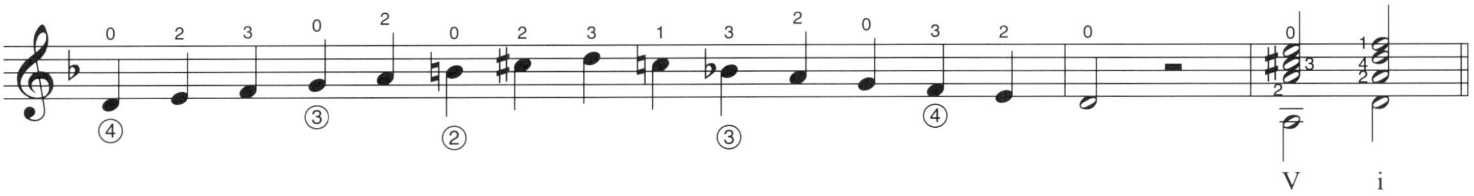

Chromatic Scale

Beginning on D (1 octave)

Tremolando Scales

Play all the single-note diatonic scales illustrated above in tremolando, with both rest stroke and free stroke, at or beyond the tempo given in the chart. Follow the left-hand fingering precisely and finish each scale with the given cadence. Play each scale with the note values and the right-hand fingering listed in the chart. See "Accent and Fingering Patterns" on p. 5.

Keys	Tempo	Note Values	RH Fingering
G, D, F major E, B, D minor (harmonic and melodic)	♩ = 88	♫♫	*im* or *mi* *ma* or *am*

Arpeggio Patterns

Play the following arpeggio patterns at or beyond the given tempo. Use the given fingering and observe the repeat signs.

1. *p–m–i* triplet pattern

♩ = 72

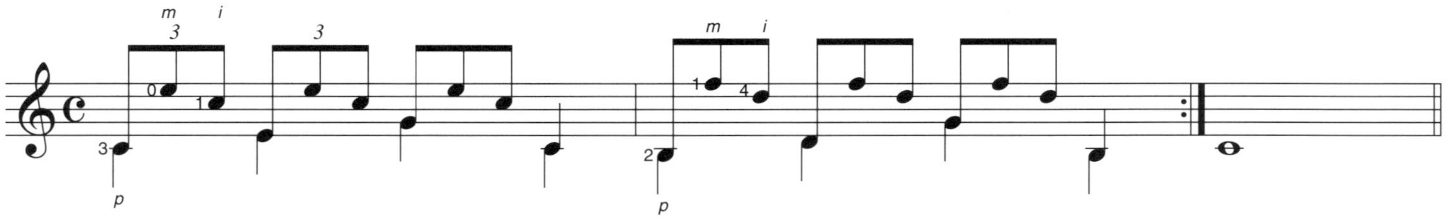

2. *p–i–m* triplet pattern

♩ = 72

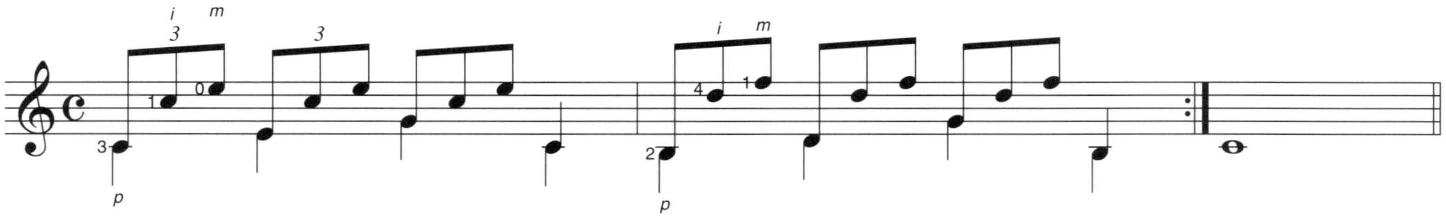

3. *p–a–i* triplet pattern

♩ = 72

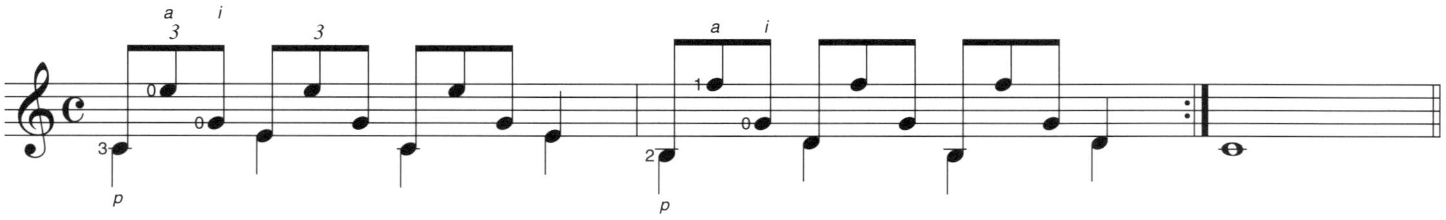

4. *p–i–a* triplet pattern

♩ = 72

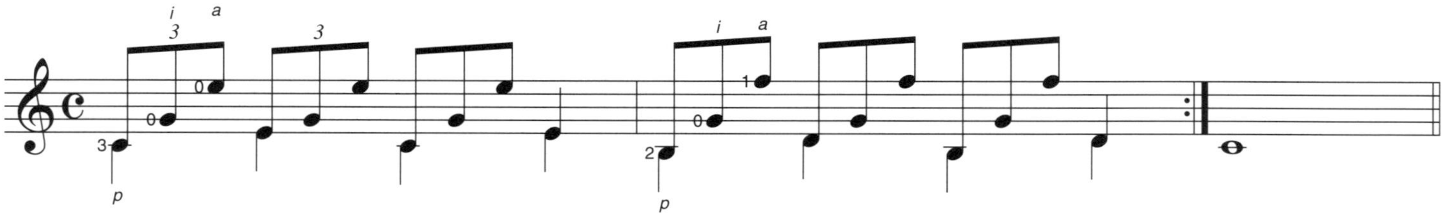

5. *p–i–m–i* pattern

♩ = 60

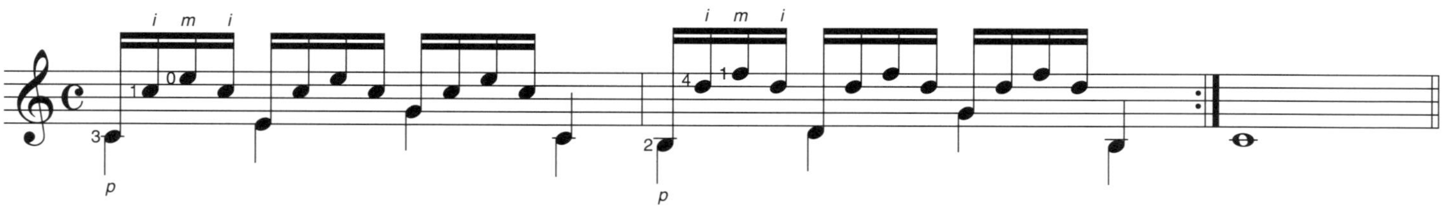

Level 2

Diatonic and Chromatic Scales

Play the following scales, in both rest stroke and free stroke, at or beyond the tempo given in the chart. Follow the left-hand fingering precisely and finish each diatonic scale with the given cadence. Play each scale with the note values and the right-hand fingering listed in the chart. See "Accent and Fingering Patterns" on p. 5.

	Keys	Tempo	Note Values	RH Fingering
Diatonic	C, G, A major A, E, F♯ minor (harmonic and melodic)	♩ = 120	♩	*im* or *mi* *ma* or *am*
Chromatic	Beginning on A			

Diatonic Scales

C Major (1 octave)

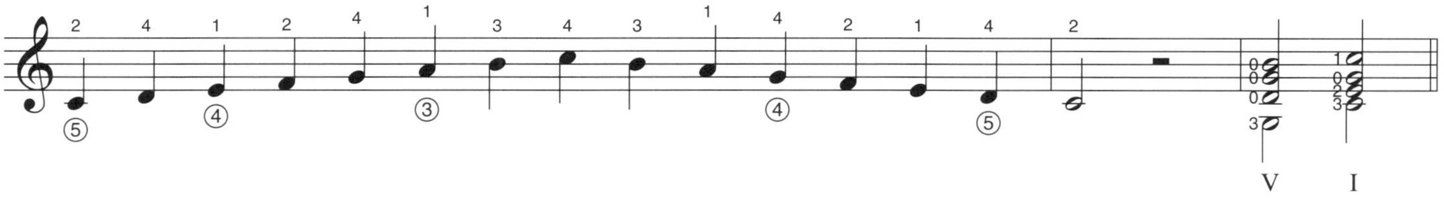

A Minor Harmonic (2 octaves)

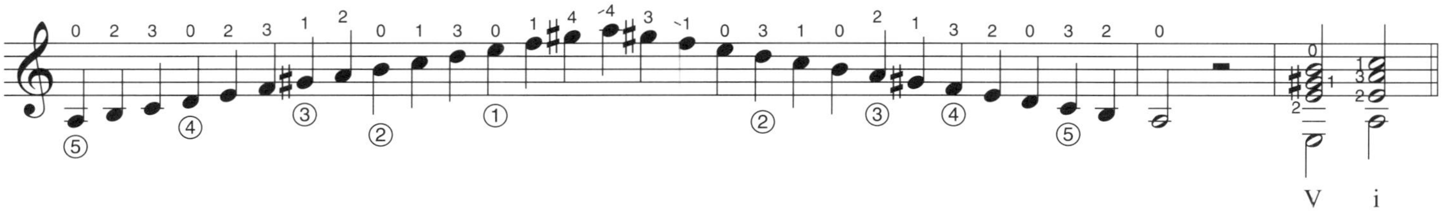

A Minor Melodic (2 octaves)

G Major (1 octave)

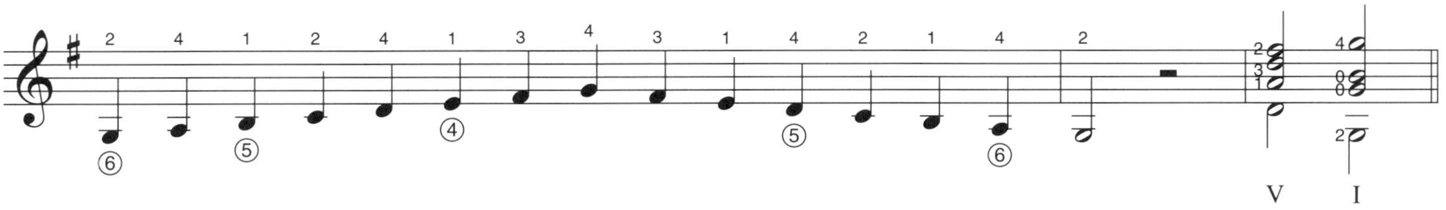

E Minor Harmonic (1 octave)

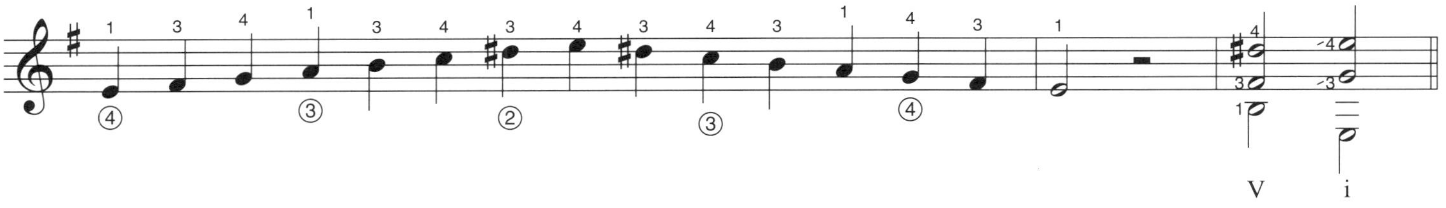

E Minor Melodic (1 octave)

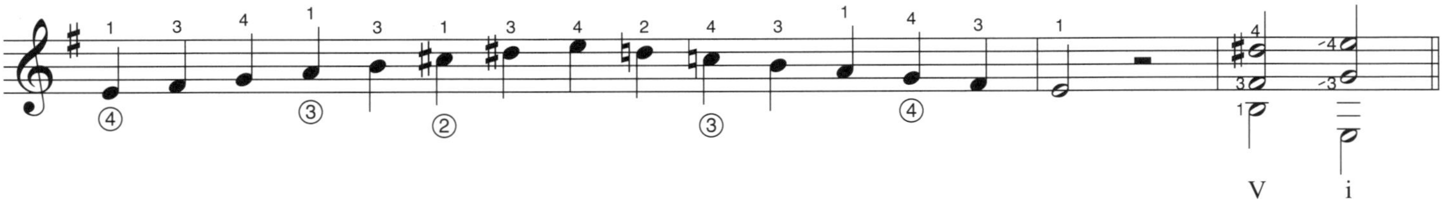

A Major (1 octave)

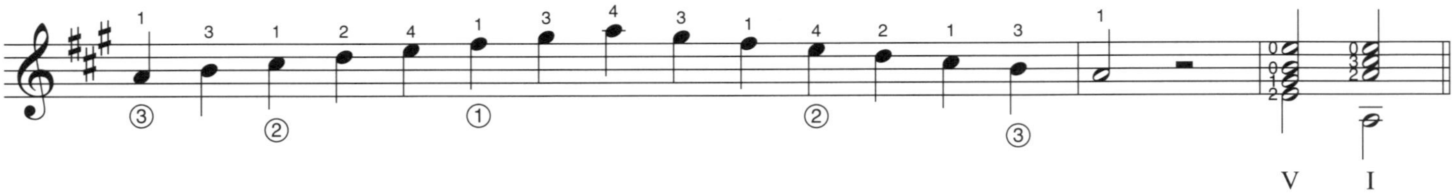

F♯ Minor Harmonic (1 octave)

F♯ Minor Melodic (1 octave)

Chromatic Scale

Beginning on A (1 octave)

Tremolando Scales

Play all the single-note diatonic scales illustrated above in tremolando, with both rest stroke and free stroke, at or beyond the tempo given in the chart. Follow the left-hand fingering precisely and finish each scale with the given cadence. Play each scale with the note values and the right-hand fingering listed in the chart. See "Accent and Fingering Patterns" on p. 5.

Keys	Tempo	Note Values	RH Fingering
C, G, A major A, E, F♯ minor (harmonic and melodic)	♩ = 96		*im* or *mi* *ma* or *am*

Arpeggio Patterns

Play the following arpeggio patterns at or beyond the given tempo. Use the given fingering and observe the repeat signs.

1. *p–m–i* triplet pattern

♩ = 76

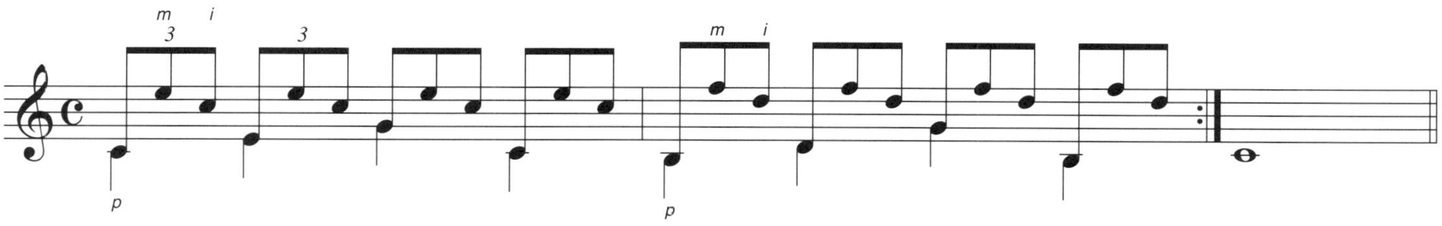

2. *p–i–m* triplet pattern

♩ = 76

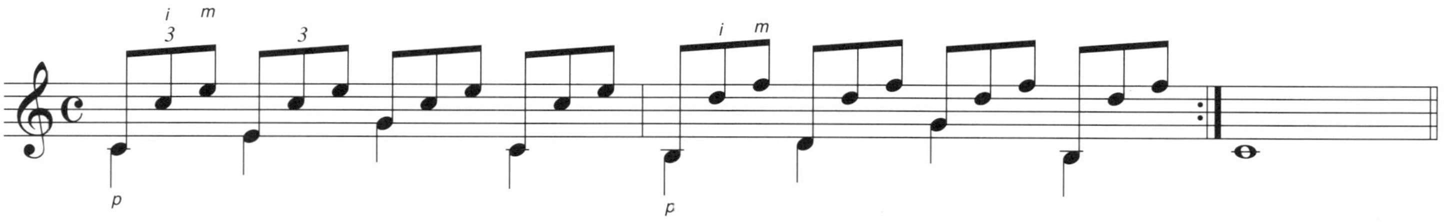

3. *p–a–i* triplet pattern

♩ = 76

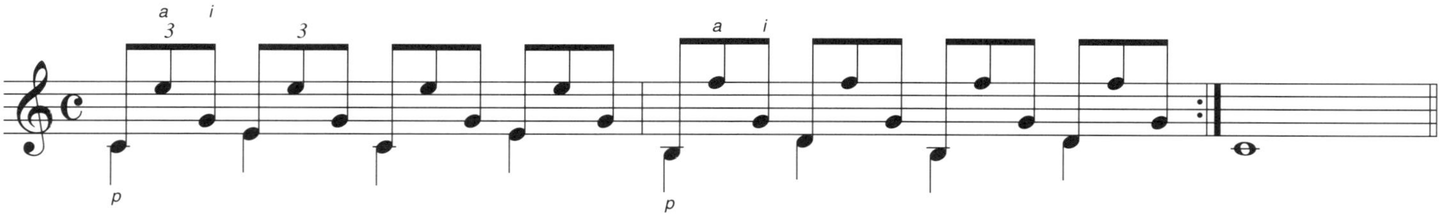

4. *p–i–a* triplet pattern

♩ = 76

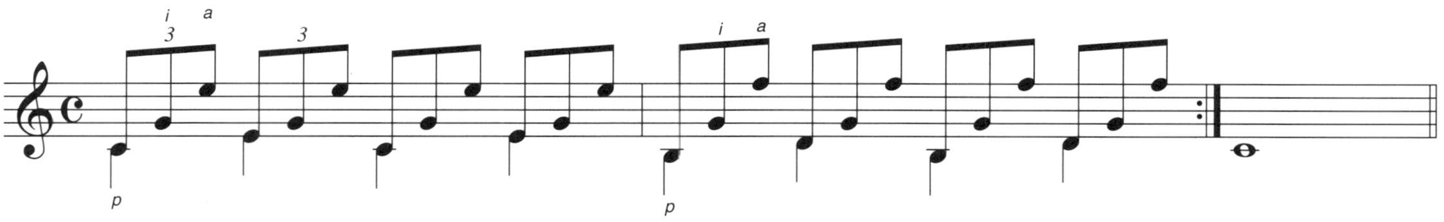

5. *p–i–a–p–i–m* triplet pattern

♩ = 76

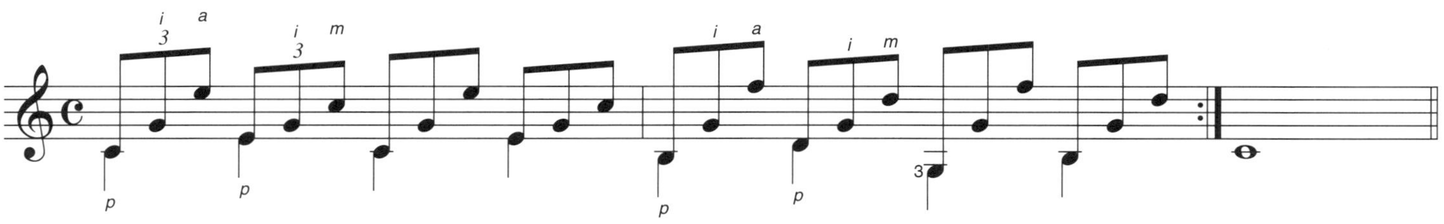

6. *p–a–i–p–m–i* triplet pattern

♩ = 76

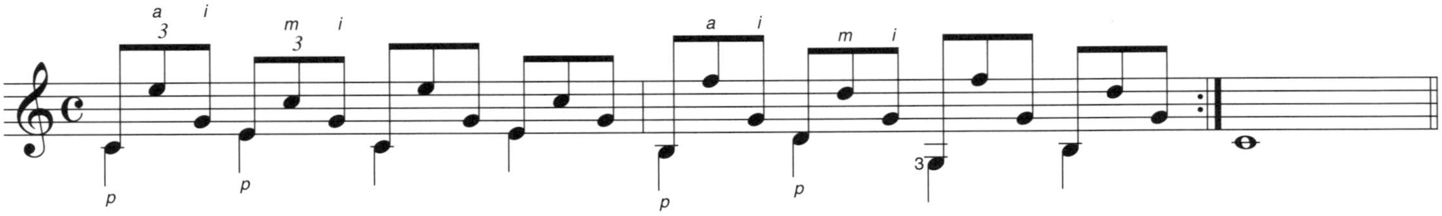

7. *p–i–m–a* ascending pattern

♩ = 66

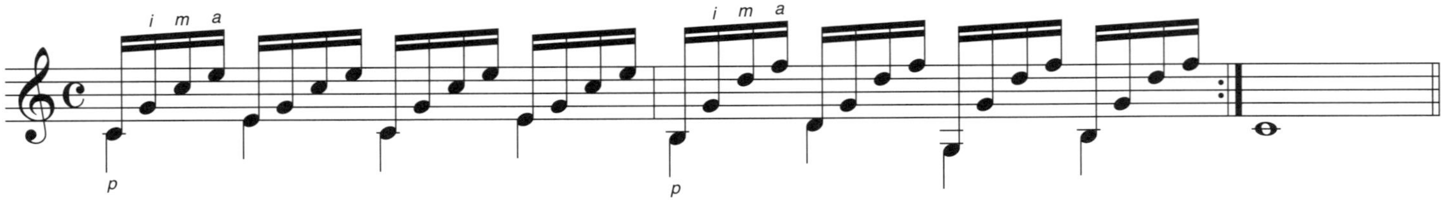

8. *p–a–m–i* descending pattern

♩ = 66

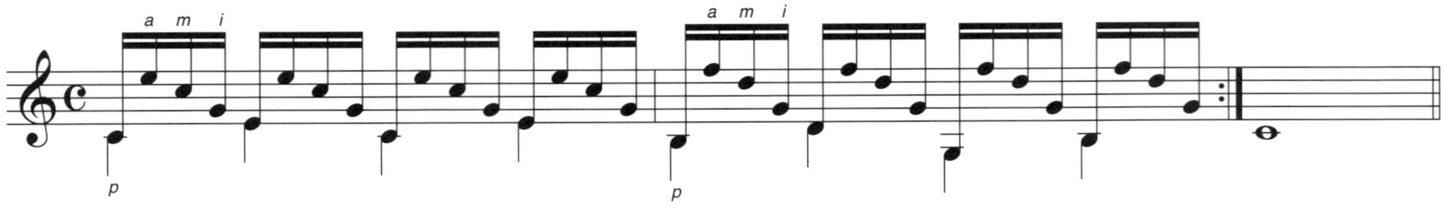

9. *p–i–m–i* pattern

♩ = 63

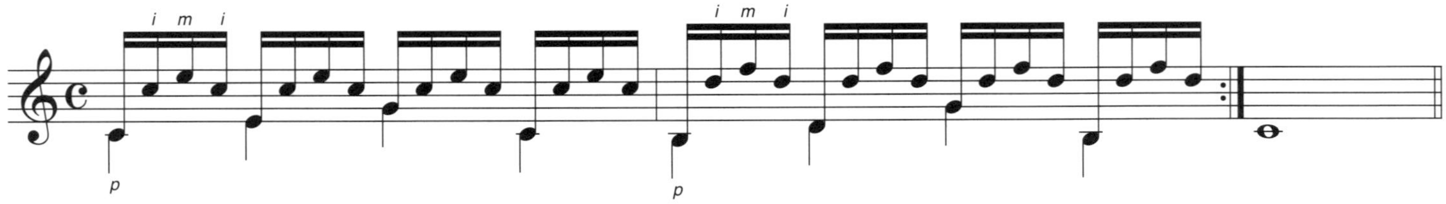

Level 3

Diatonic and Chromatic Scales

Play the following scales, in both rest stroke and free stroke, at or beyond the tempo given in the chart. Follow the left-hand fingering precisely and finish each diatonic scale with the given cadence. Play each scale with the note values and the right-hand fingering listed in the chart. See "Accent and Fingering Patterns" on p. 5.

	Keys	Tempo	Note Values	RH Fingering
Diatonic	D, E, B♭ major B, C♯, G minor (harmonic and melodic)	♩ = 69	♫	*im* or *mi* *ma* or *am*
Chromatic	Beginning on A			

Diatonic Scales

D Major (1 octave)

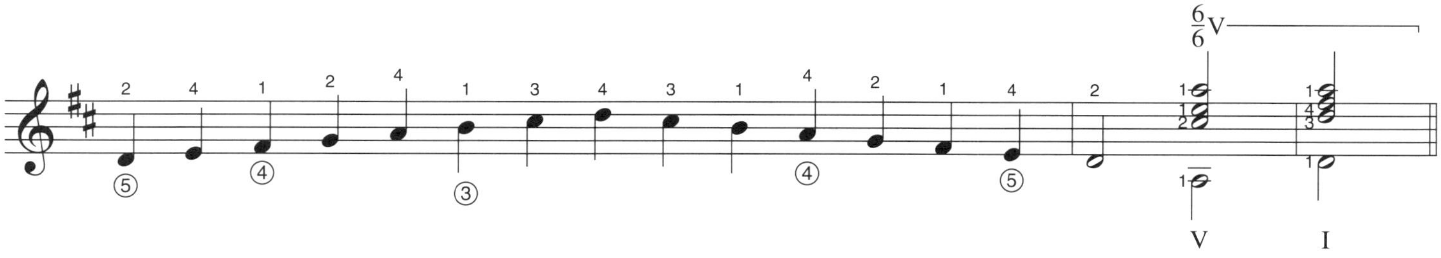

B Minor Harmonic (1 octave)

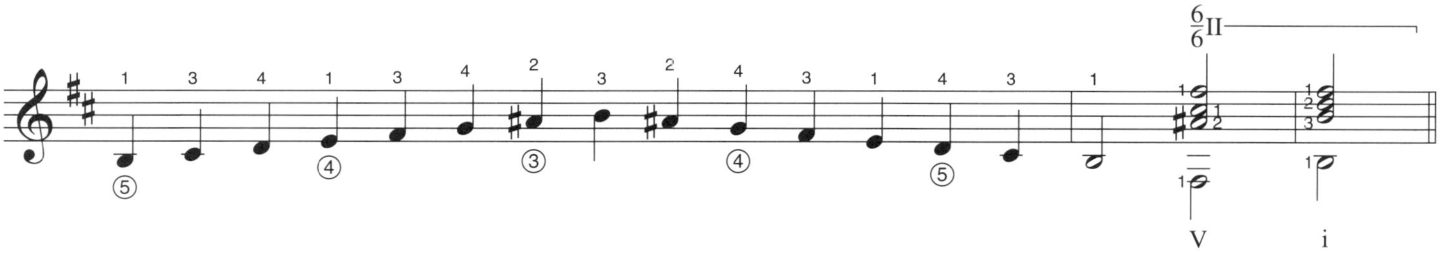

B Minor Melodic (1 octave)

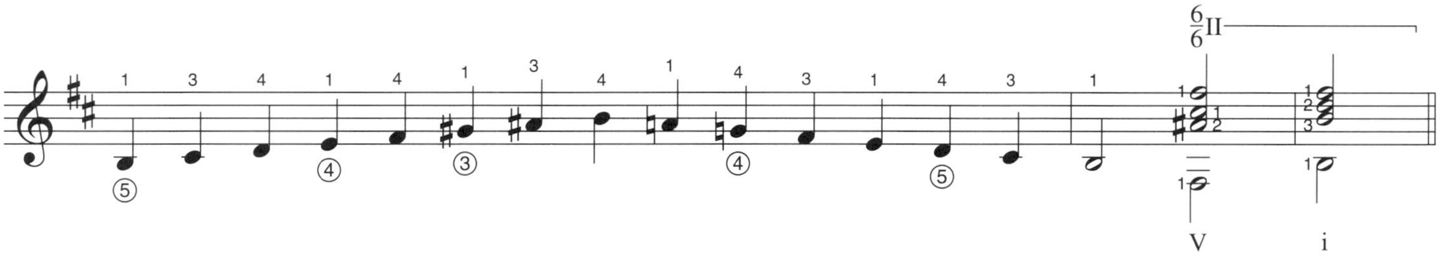

E Major (2 octaves)

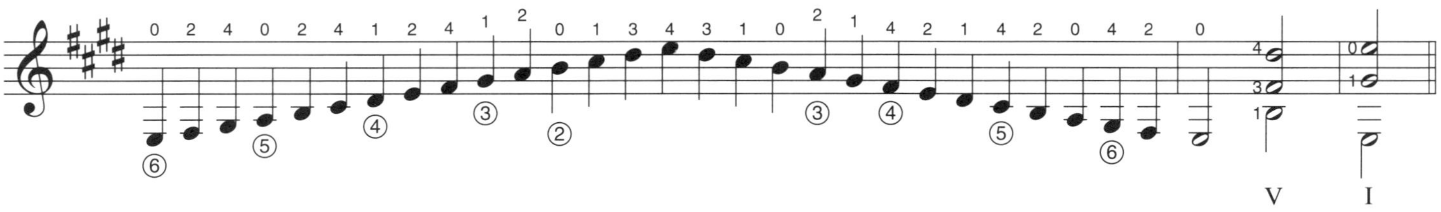

C♯ Minor Harmonic (1 octave)

C♯ Minor Melodic (1 octave)

B♭ Major (1 octave)

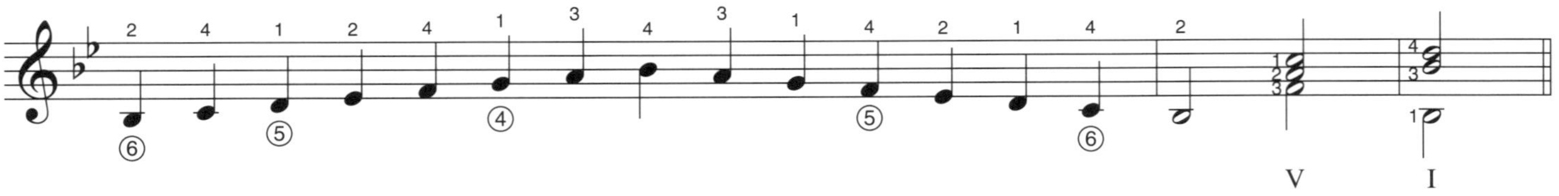

G Minor Harmonic (2 octaves)

G Minor Melodic (2 octaves)

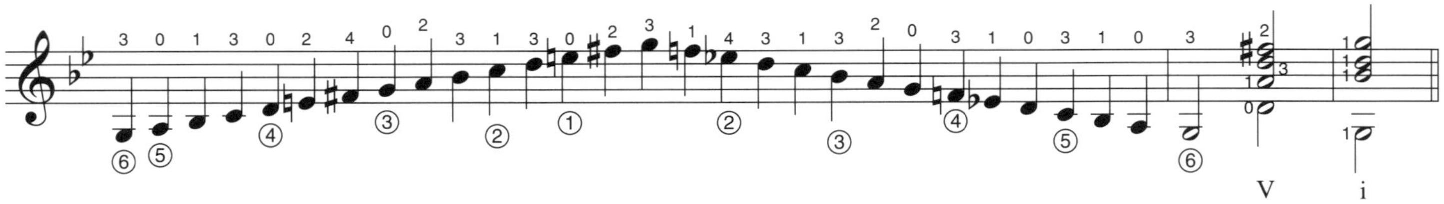

Chromatic Scale

Beginning on A (2 octaves)

Tremolando Scales

Play all the single-note diatonic scales illustrated above in tremolando, with both rest stroke and free stroke, at or beyond the tempo given in the chart. Follow the left-hand fingering precisely and finish each scale with the given cadence. Play each scale with the note values and the right-hand fingering listed in the chart. See "Accent and Fingering Patterns" on p. 5.

Keys	Tempo	Note Values	RH Fingering
D, E, B♭ major B, C♯, G minor (harmonic and melodic)	♩ = 108		*im* or *mi* *ma* or *am*

Arpeggio Patterns

Play the following arpeggio patterns at or beyond the given tempo. Use the given fingering and observe the repeat signs.

1. *p–a–i* triplet pattern

♩ = 80

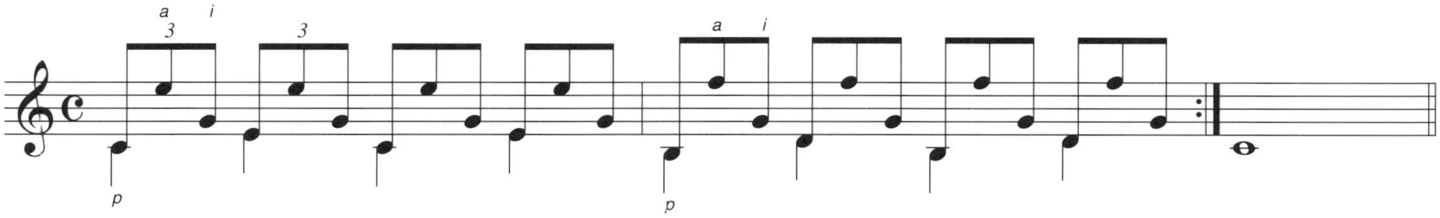

2. *p–i–a* triplet pattern

♩ = 80

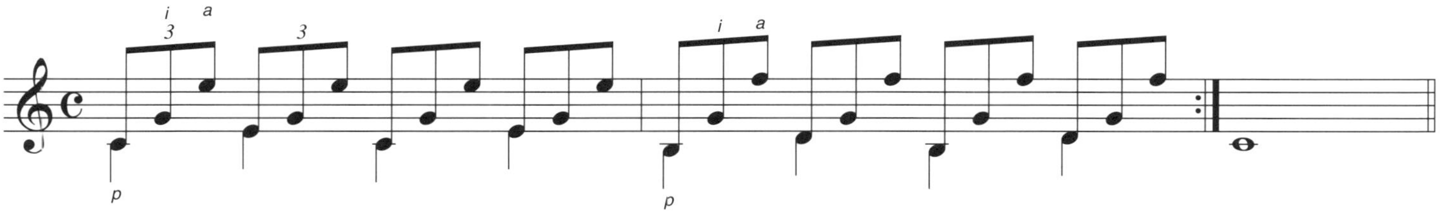

3. *p–i–a–p–i–m* triplet pattern

♩ = 80

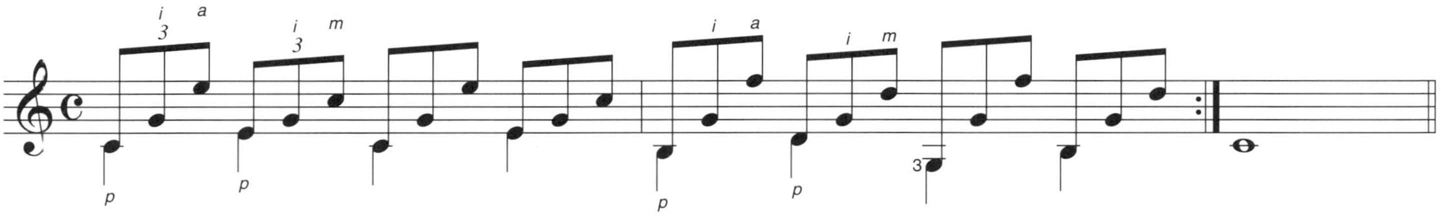

4. *p–a–i–p–m–i* triplet pattern

♩ = 80

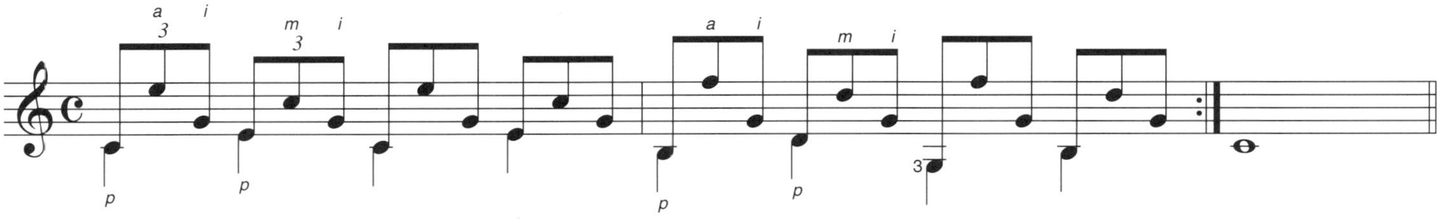

5. *p–i–m–a* ascending pattern

♩ = 69

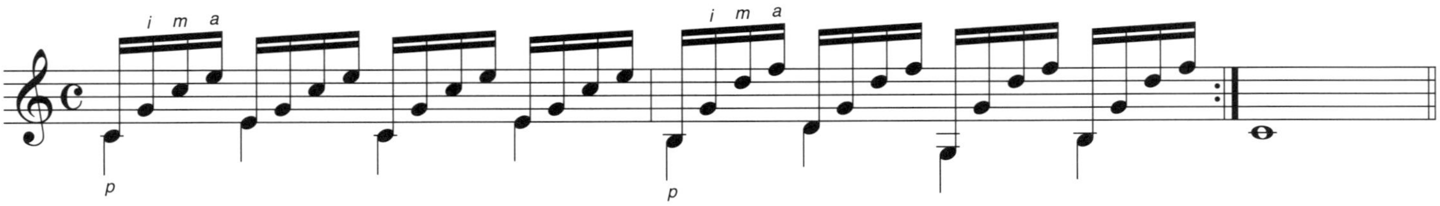

6. *p–a–m–i* descending pattern

♩ = 69

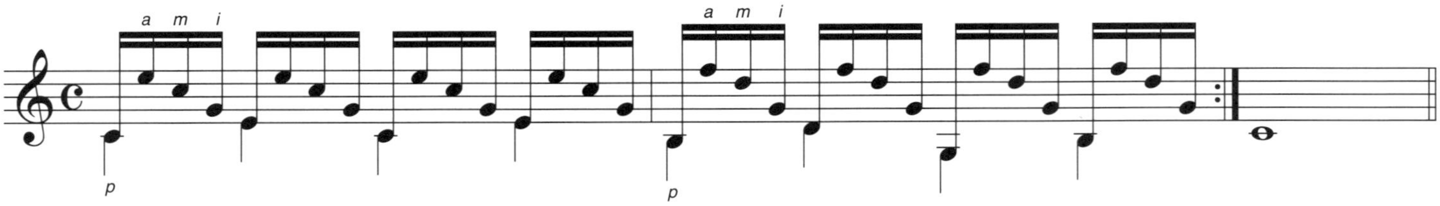

7. *p–i–m–i* pattern

♩ = 69

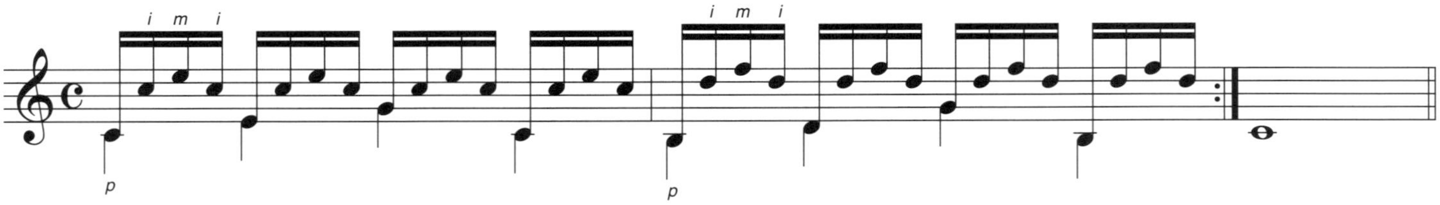

8. *p–m–i–m* pattern

♩ = 69

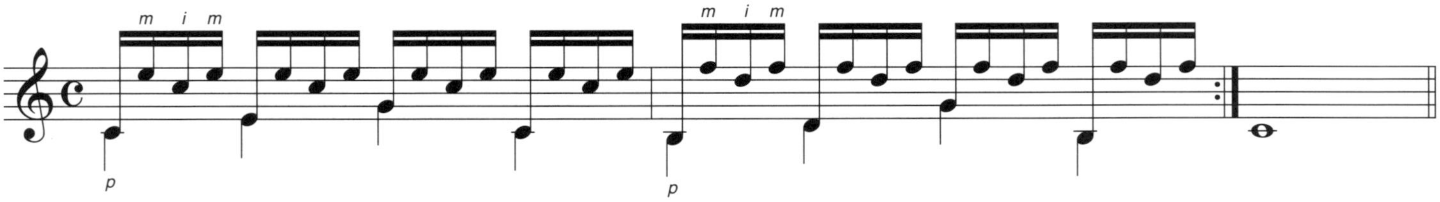

9. *p–a* dyad–*m–i* triplet pattern

♩ = 69

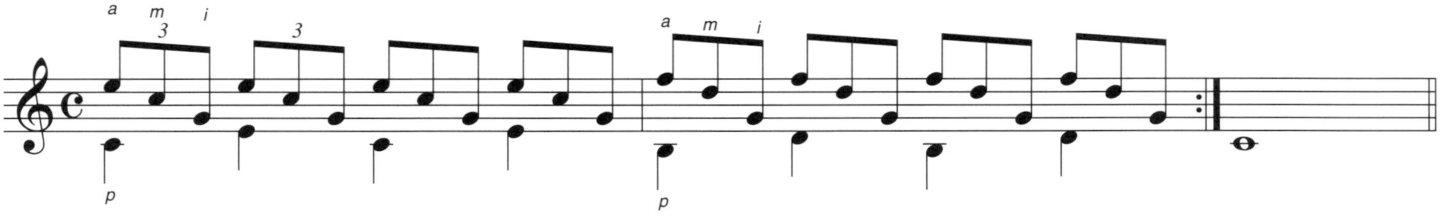

Level 4

Diatonic and Chromatic Scales

Play the following scales, in both rest stroke and free stroke, at or beyond the tempo given in the chart. Follow the left-hand fingering precisely and finish each diatonic scale with the given cadence. Play each scale with the note values and the right-hand fingering listed in the chart. See "Accent and Fingering Patterns" on p. 5.

	Keys	Tempo	Note Values	RH Fingering
Diatonic	C, F♯, E♭, A♭ major A, D♯, C, F minor (harmonic and melodic)	♩ = 69	♫ and ♪♪♪ (3)	*im* or *mi* *ma* or *am*
Chromatic	Beginning on B			

Diatonic Scales

C Major (2 octaves)

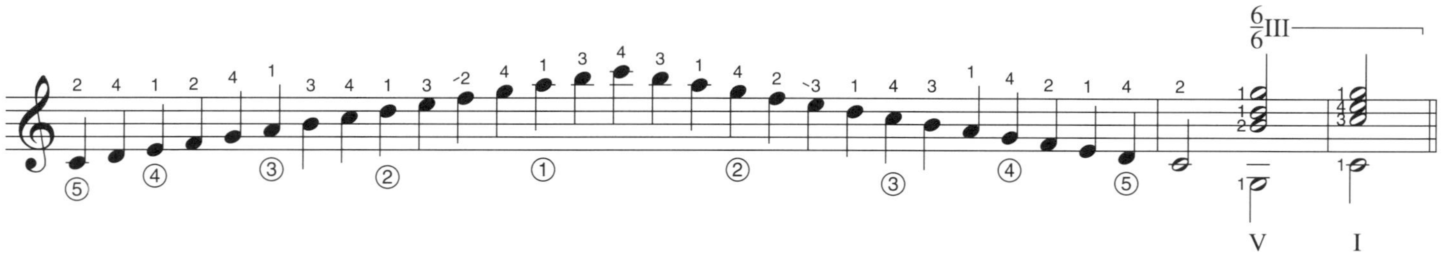

A Minor Harmonic (2 octaves)

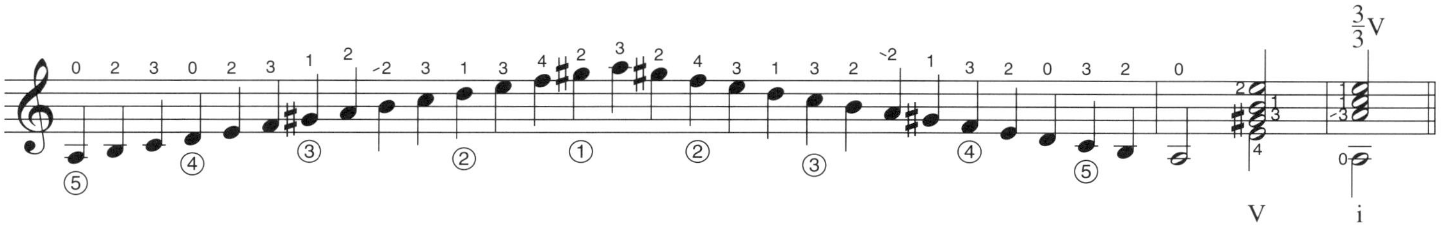

A Minor Melodic (2 octaves)

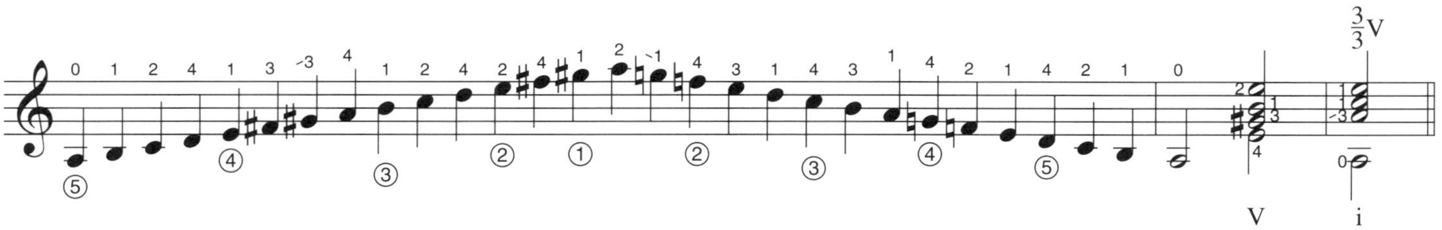

F♯ Major (2 octaves)

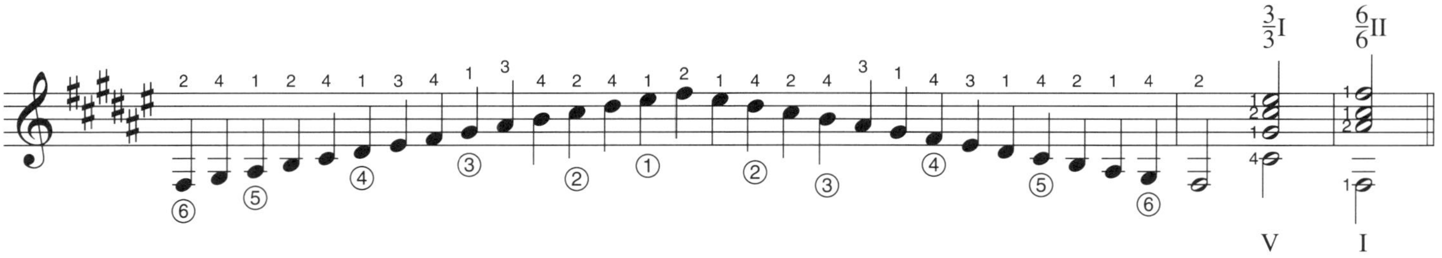

D♯ Minor Harmonic (1 octave)

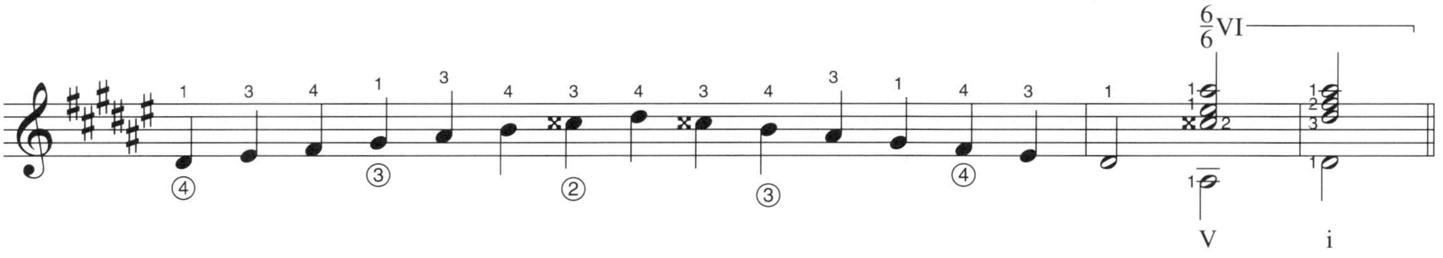

D♯ Minor Melodic (1 octave)

E♭ Major (1 octave)

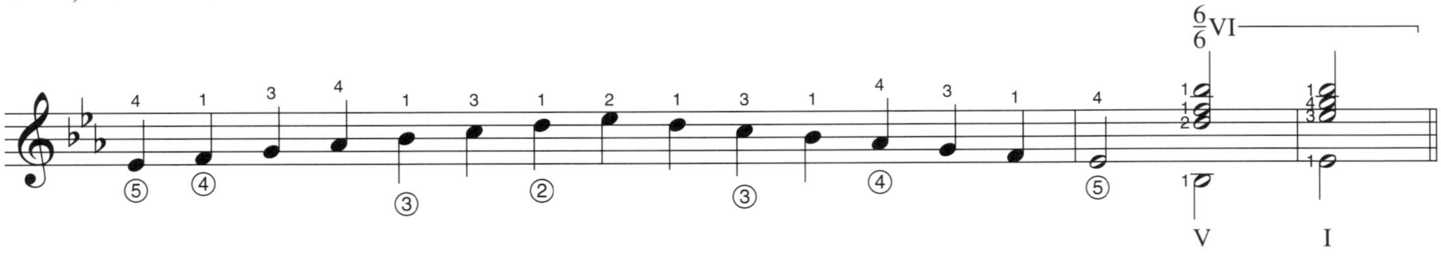

C Minor Harmonic (1 octave)

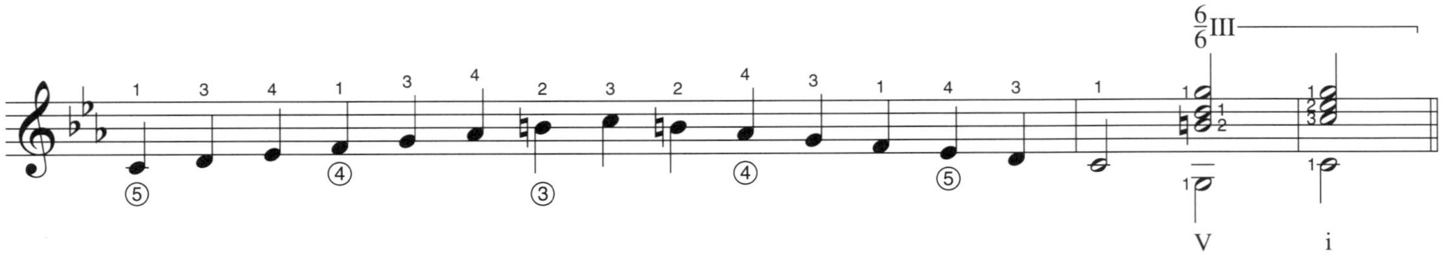

C Minor Melodic (1 octave)

A♭ Major (1 octave)

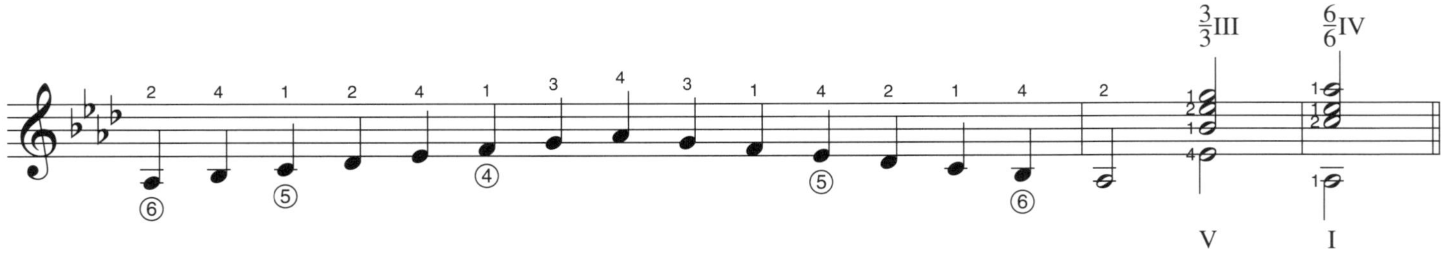

F Minor Harmonic (1 octave)

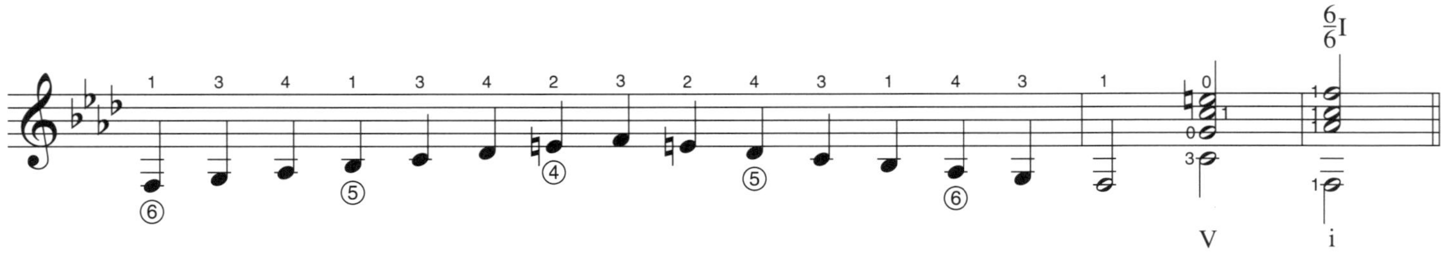

F Minor Melodic (1 octave)

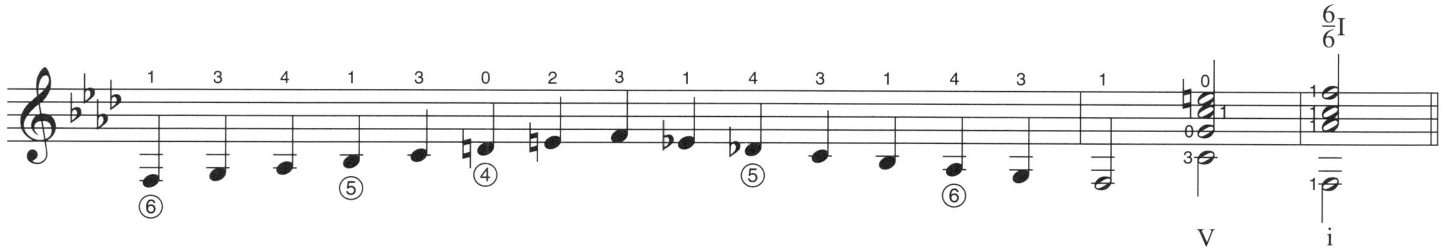

Chromatic Scale

Beginning on B (2 octaves)

Tremolando Scales

Play all the single-note diatonic scales illustrated above in tremolando, with both rest stroke and free stroke, at or beyond the tempo given in the chart. Follow the left-hand fingering precisely and finish each scale with the given cadence. Play each scale with the note values and the right-hand fingering listed in the chart. See "Accent and Fingering Patterns" on p. 5.

Keys	Tempo	Note Values	RH Fingering
C, F♯, E♭, A♭ major A, D♯ C, F minor (harmonic and melodic)	♩ = 60	♬♬ (four sixteenth notes)	*im* or *mi* *ma* or *am*

Slur Scale

Play the following scale at or beyond the given tempo. Follow the left-hand fingering precisely; any right-hand fingering is acceptable.

D Major, single slurs (1 octave)

♩ = 56

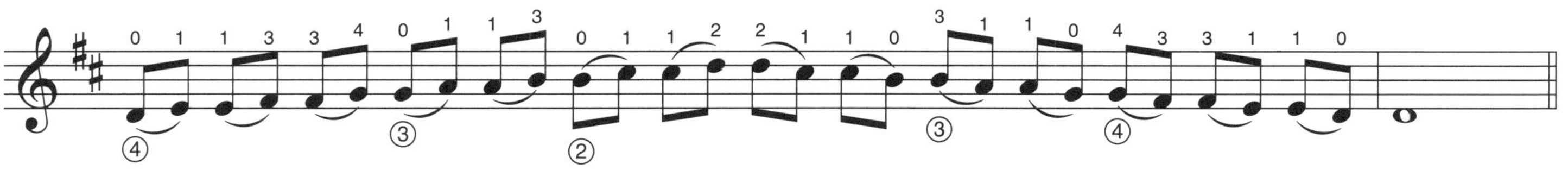

Arpeggio Patterns

Play the following arpeggio patterns at or beyond the given tempo. Use the given fingering and observe the repeat signs.

1. *p–i–a–p–i–m* triplet pattern

♩ = 84

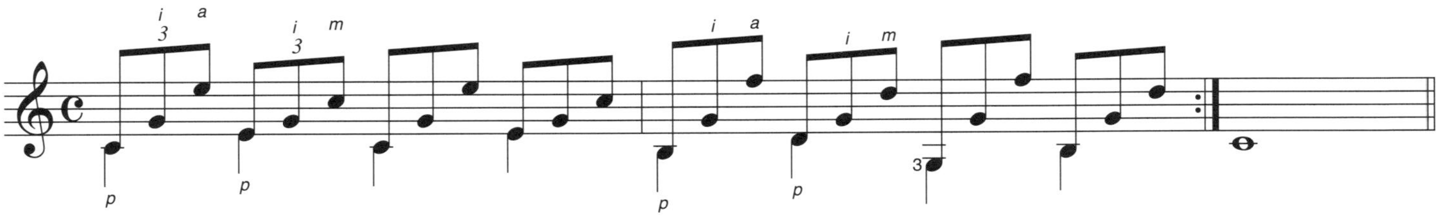

2. *p–a–i–p–m–i* triplet pattern

♩ = 84

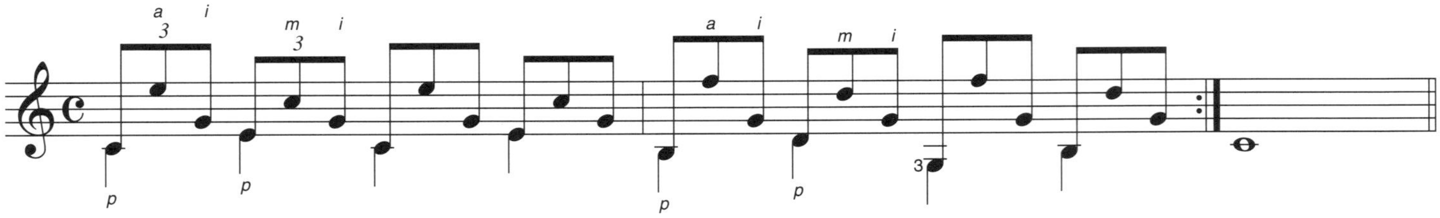

3. *p–i–m–a* ascending pattern

♩ = 72

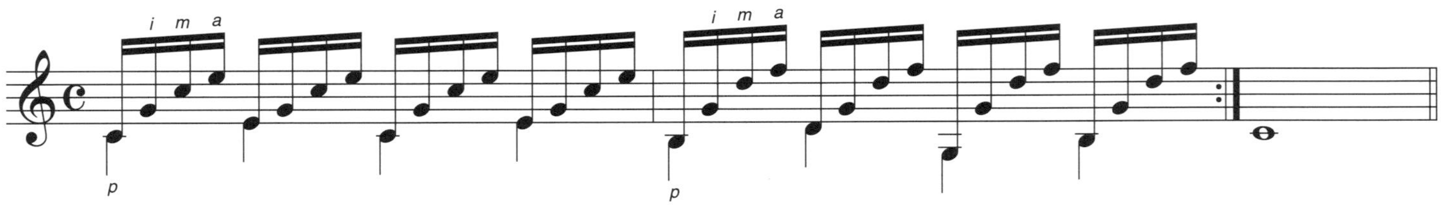

4. *p–a–m–i* descending pattern

♩ = 72

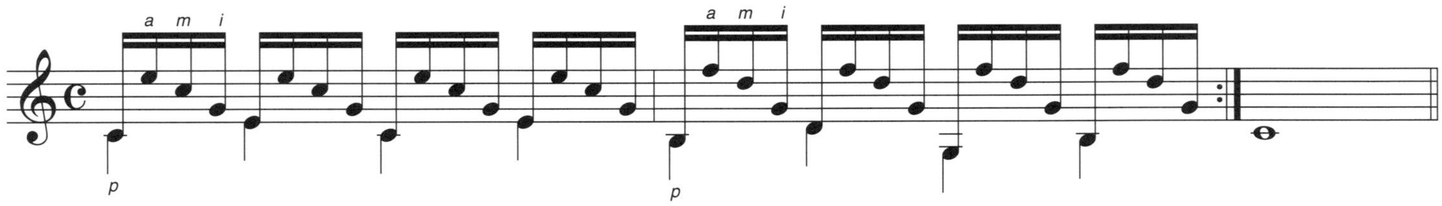

5. *p–i–m–i* pattern

♩ = 72

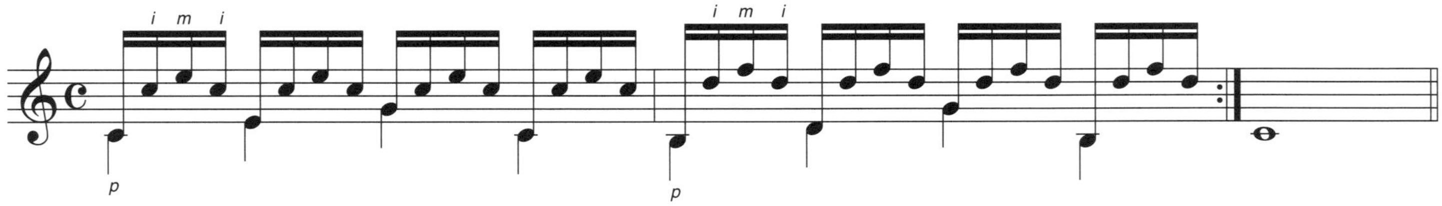

6. *p–m–i–m* pattern

♩ = 72

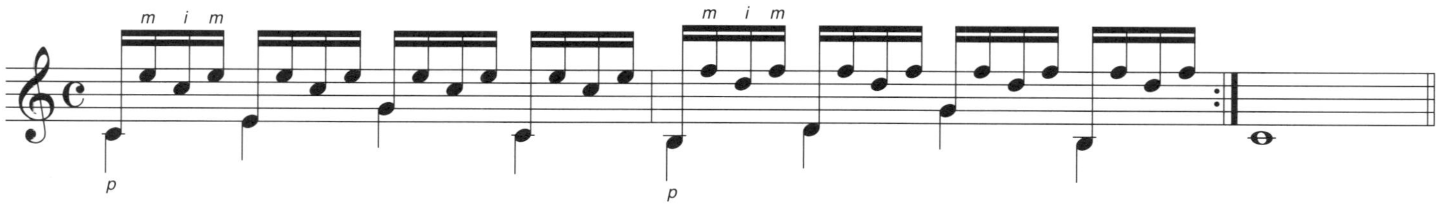

7. ascending and descending sextuplet pattern

♩ = 46

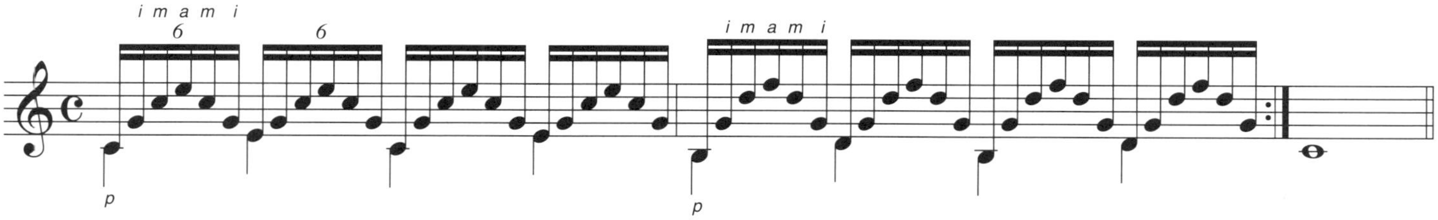

8. descending and ascending sextuplet pattern

♩ = 46

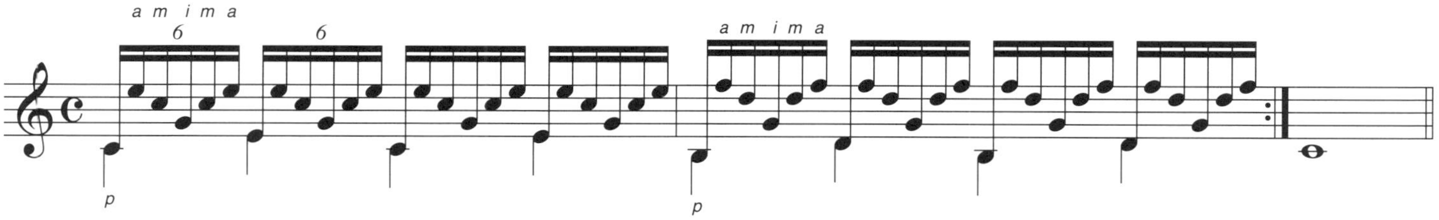

9. *p–a* dyad–*m–i* triplet pattern

♩ = 72

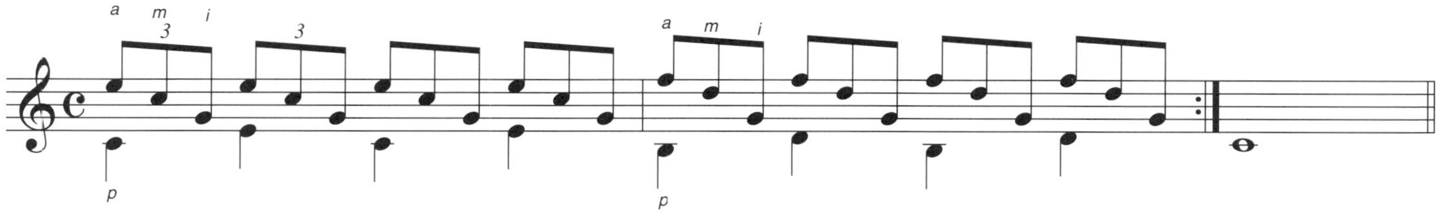

10. *p–i* dyad–*m–a* triplet pattern

♩ = 72

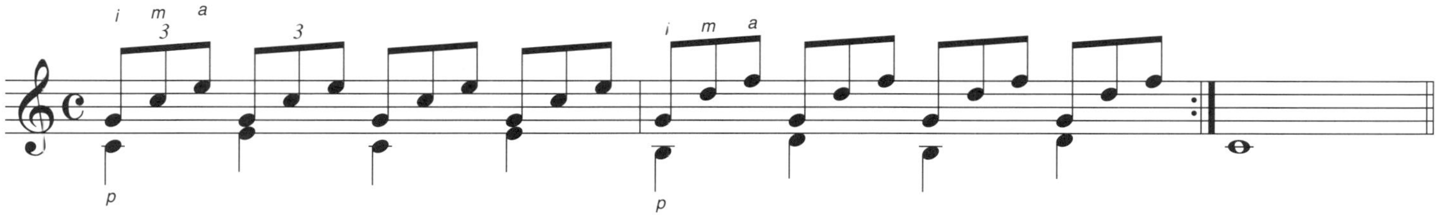

Level 5

Diatonic and Chromatic Scales

Play the following scales, in both rest stroke and free stroke, at or beyond the tempo given in the chart. Follow the left-hand fingering precisely and finish each diatonic scale with the given cadence. Play each scale with the note values and the right-hand fingering listed in the chart. See "Accent and Fingering Patterns" on p. 5.

	Keys	Tempo	Note Values	RH Fingering
Diatonic	G, D, A♭, D♭ major E, B, F, B♭ minor (harmonic and melodic)	♩ = 69	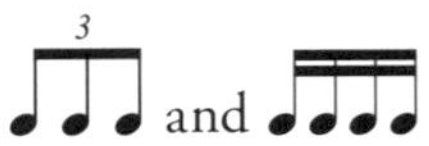	*im* or *mi* *ma* or *am* *ia* or *ai*
Chromatic	Beginning on C			

Diatonic Scales

G Major (2 octaves)

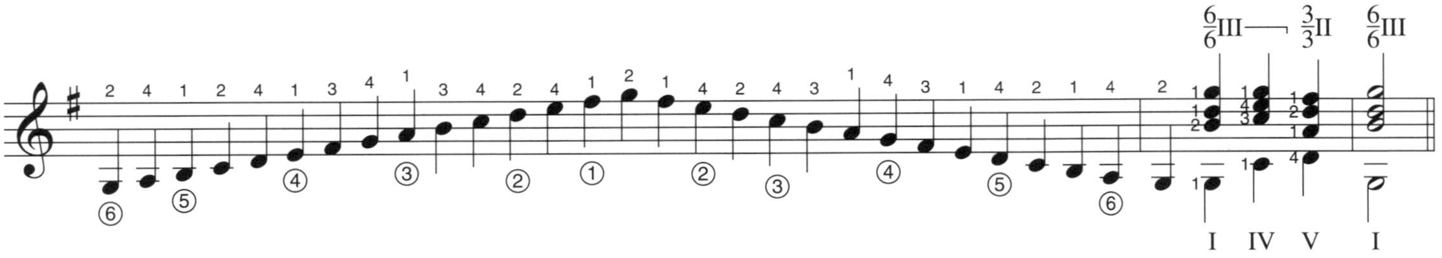

E Minor Harmonic (2 octaves)

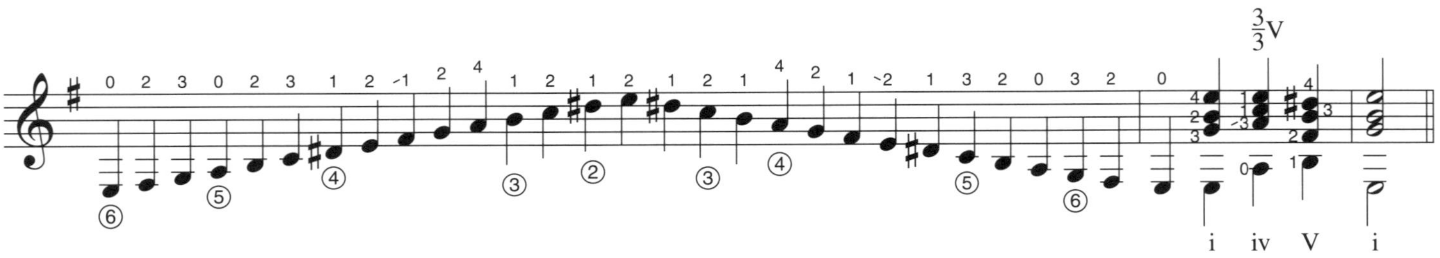

E Minor Melodic (2 octaves)

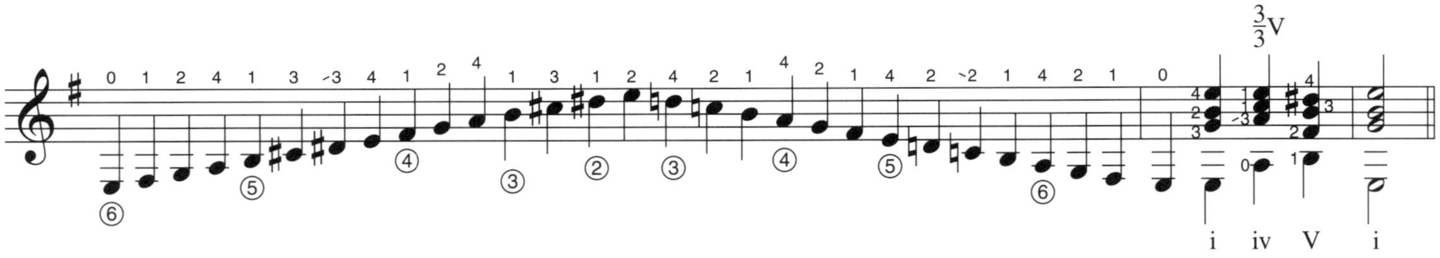

D Major (2 octaves)

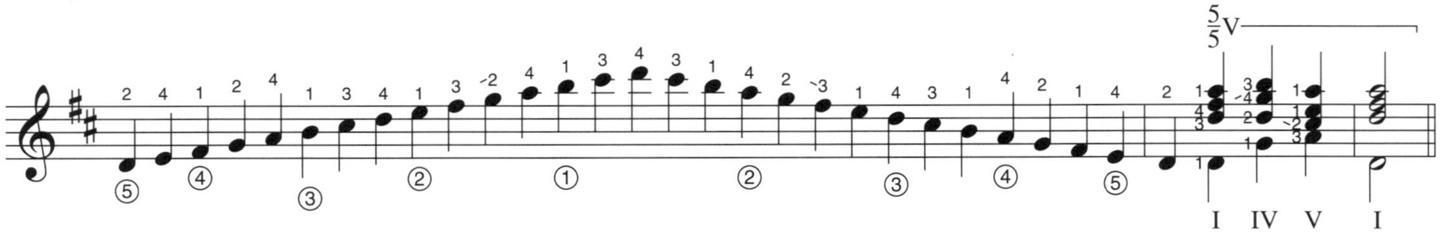

B Minor Harmonic (2 octaves)

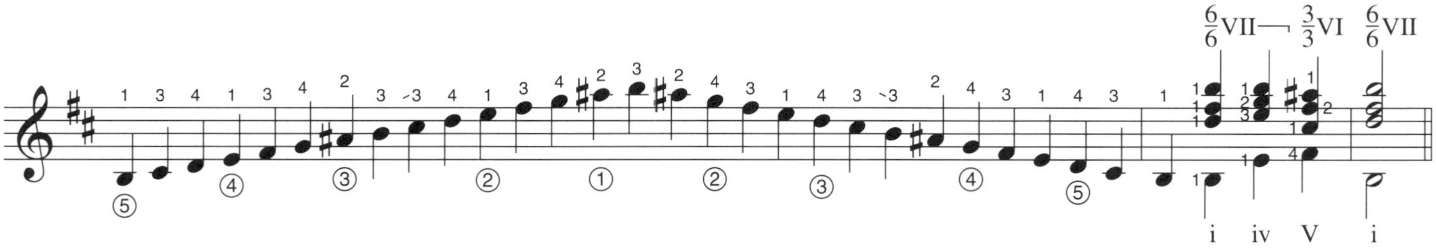

B Minor Melodic (2 octaves)

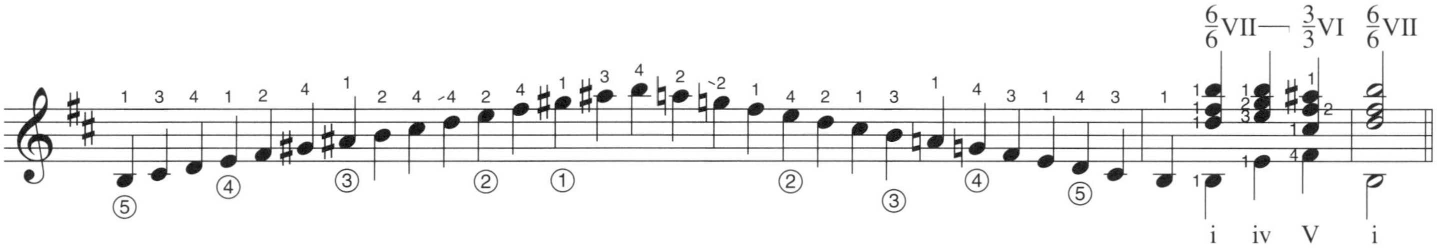

A♭ Major (2 octaves)

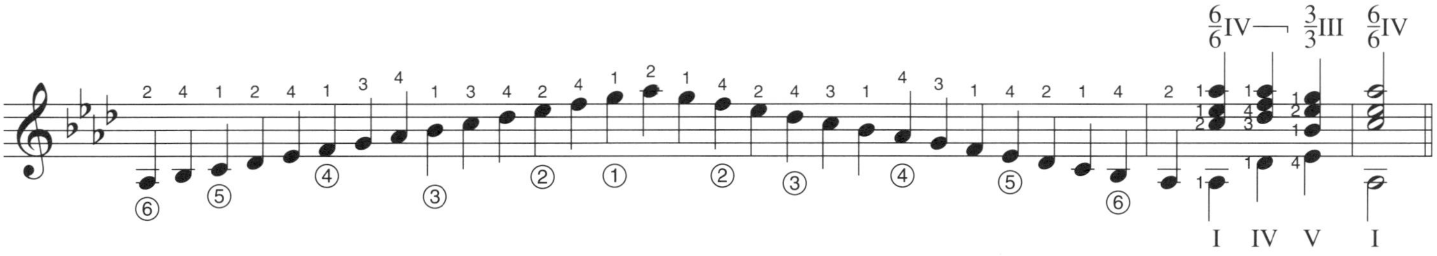

F Minor Harmonic (2 octaves)

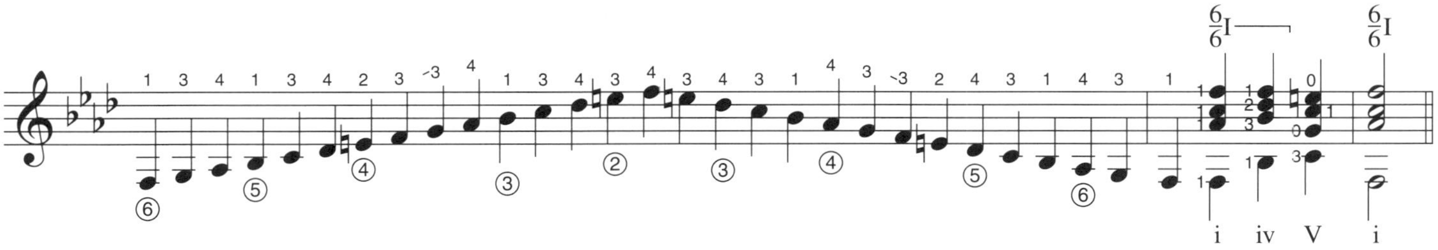

F Minor Melodic (2 octaves)

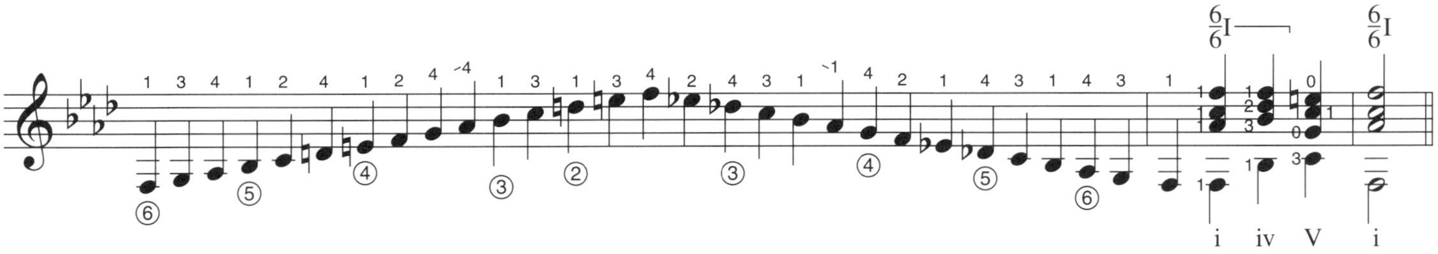

D♭ Major (1 octave)

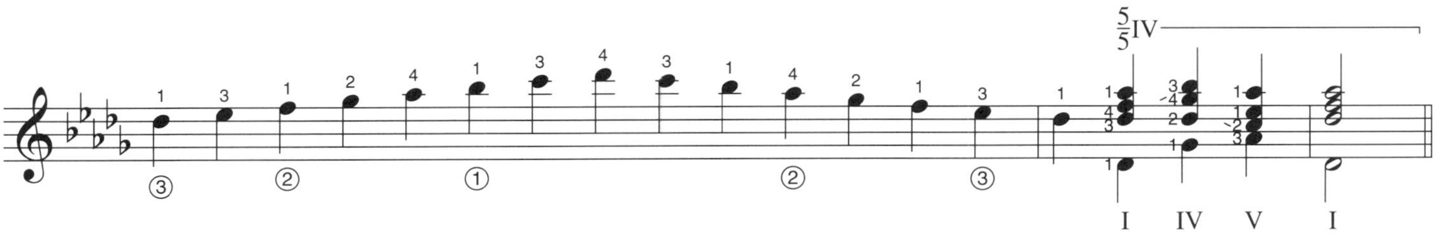

B♭ Minor Harmonic (2 octaves)

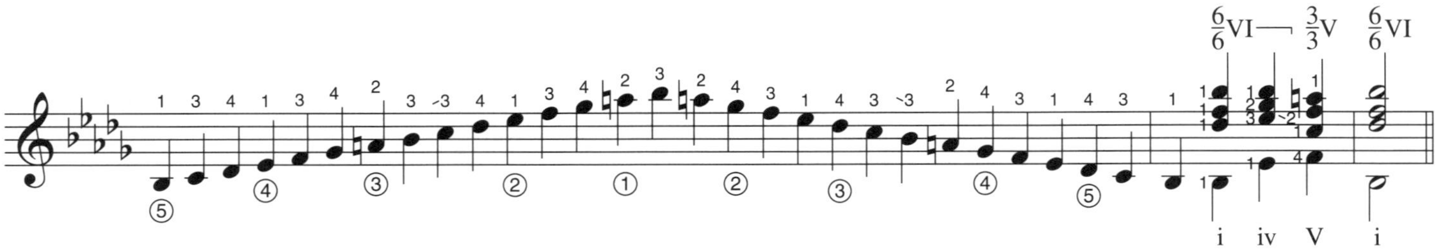

B♭ Minor Melodic (2 octaves)

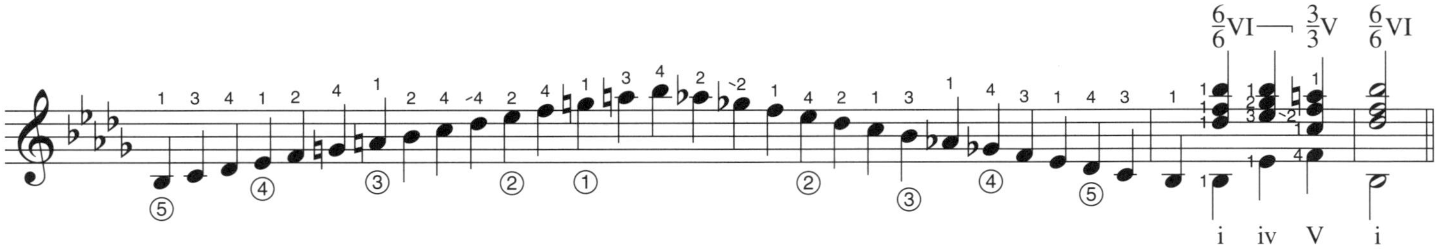

Chromatic Scale

Beginning on C (2 octaves)

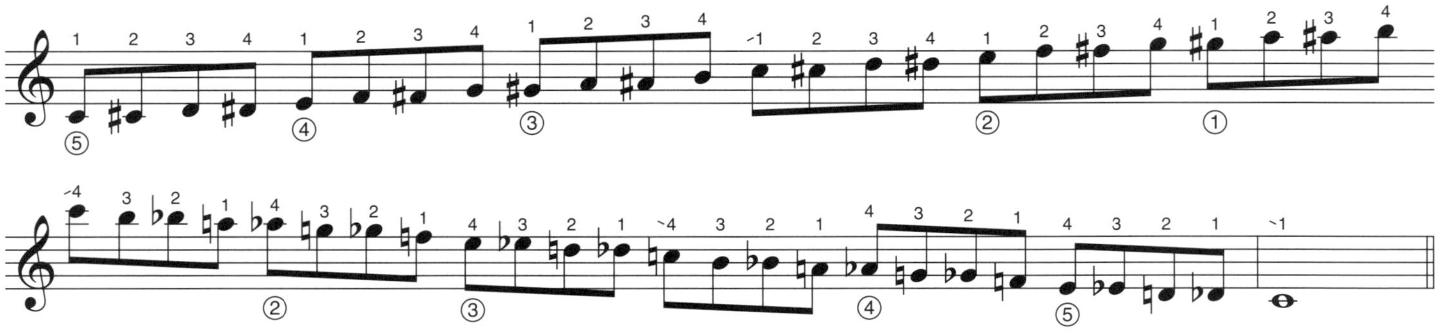

Tremolando Scales

Play all the single-note diatonic scales illustrated above in tremolando, with both rest stroke and free stroke, at or beyond the tempo given in the chart. Follow the left-hand fingering precisely and finish each scale with the given cadence. Play each scale with the note values and the right-hand fingering listed in the chart. See "Accent and Fingering Patterns" on p. 5.

Keys	Tempo	Note Values	RH Fingering
G, D, A♭, D♭ major E, B, F, B♭ minor (harmonic and melodic)	♩ = 88	♪♪♪ (3)	*im* or *mi* *ma* or *am* *ia* or *ai*

Slur Scales

Play the following scales at or beyond the given tempo. Follow the left-hand fingering precisely; any right-hand fingering is acceptable.

C Major, single slurs (1 octave)

♩ = 60

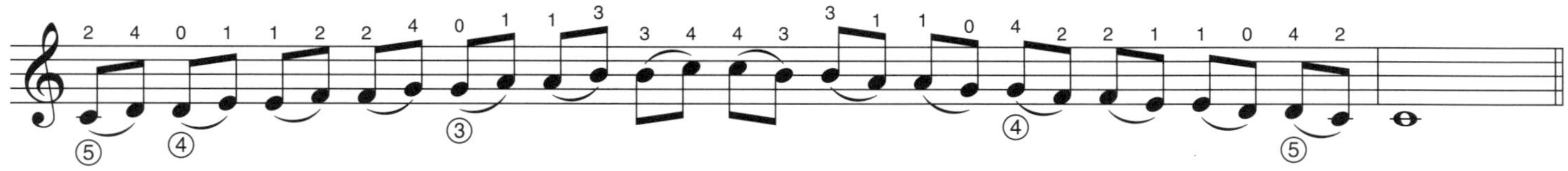

G Major, single slurs (1 octave)

♩ = 60

Arpeggio Patterns

Play the following arpeggio patterns at or beyond the given tempo. Use the given fingering and observe the repeat signs.

1. *p–i–m–a* ascending pattern

♩ = 76

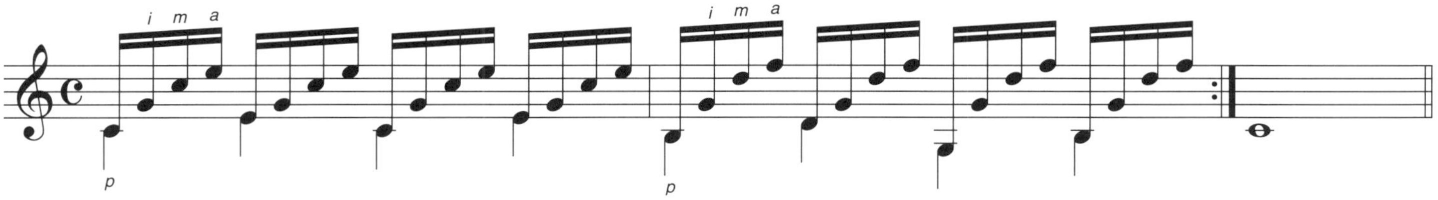

2. *p–a–m–i* descending pattern

♩ = 76

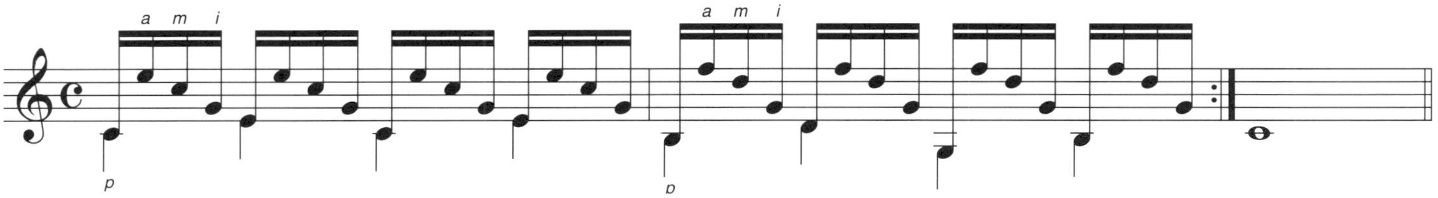

3. *p–i–m–i* pattern

♩ = 76

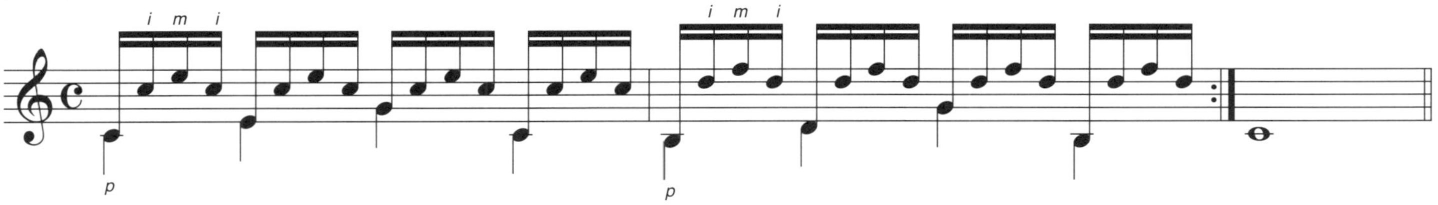

4. *p–m–i–m* pattern

♩ = 76

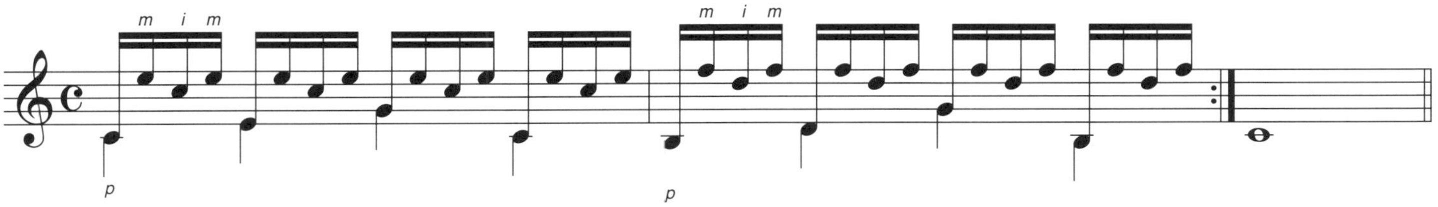

5. ascending and descending sextuplet pattern

♩ = 52

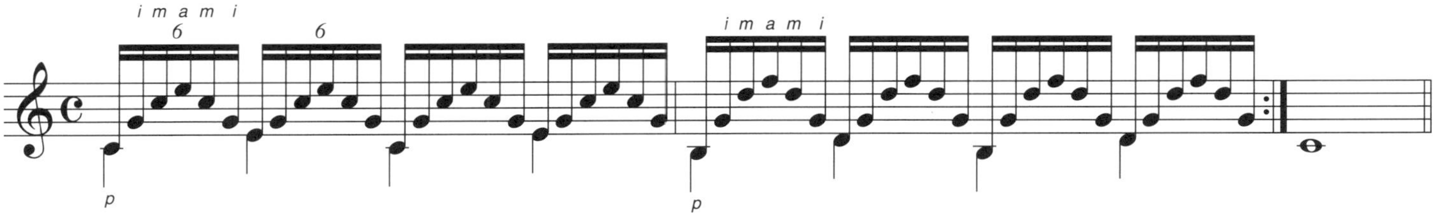

6. descending and ascending sextuplet pattern

♩ = 52

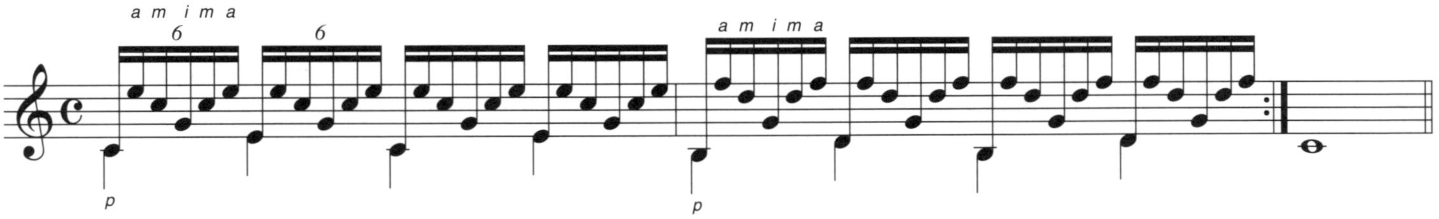

7. *p–a* dyad–*m–i* triplet pattern

♩ = 76

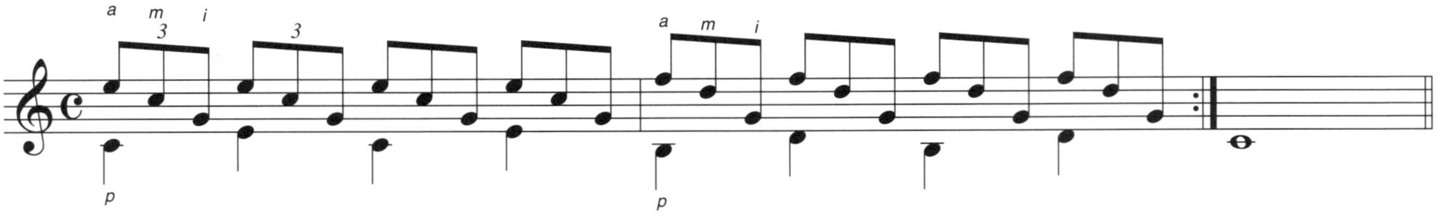

8. *p–i* dyad–*m–a* triplet pattern

♩ = 76

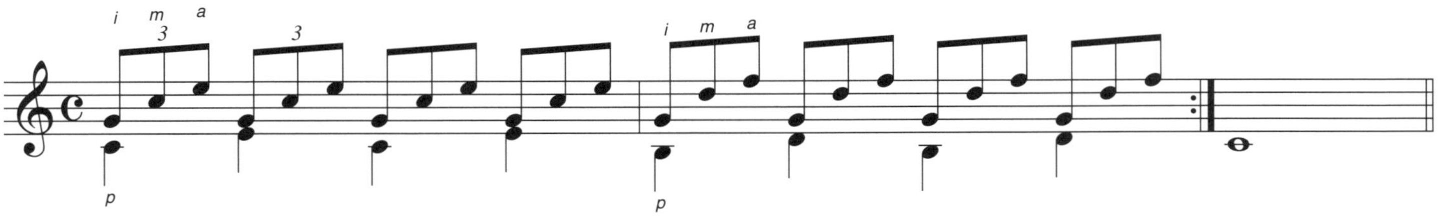

9. *p–m* dyad–*i–a* triplet pattern

♩ = 76

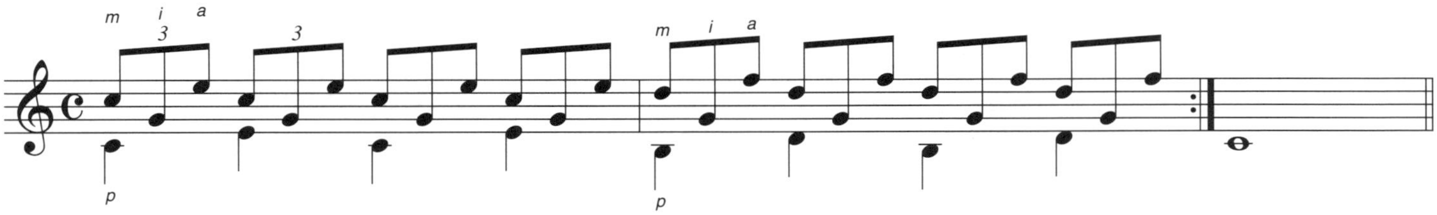

10. *p–i* dyad–*a–m* triplet pattern

♩ = 76

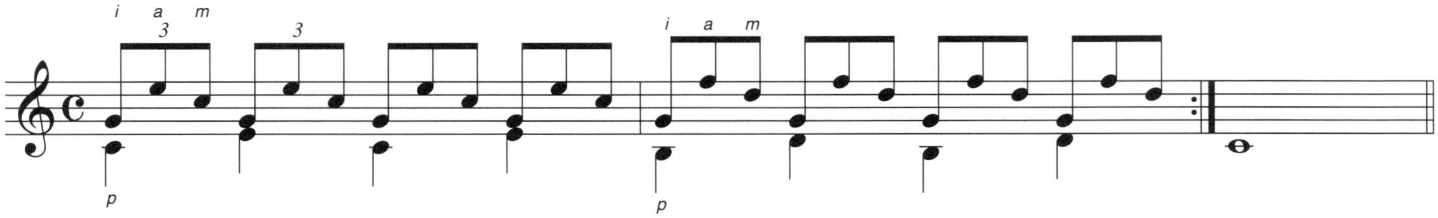

Level 6

Diatonic and Chromatic Scales

Play the following scales, in both rest stroke and free stroke, at or beyond the tempo given in the chart. Follow the left-hand fingering precisely and finish each diatonic scale with the given cadence. Play each scale with the note values and the right-hand fingering listed in the chart. See "Accent and Fingering Patterns" on p. 5.

	Keys	Tempo	Note Values	RH Fingering
Diatonic	E, B, F♯, F, B♭ major C♯, G♯, D♯, D, G minor (harmonic and melodic)	♩ = 76	[eighth-note triplet] and [four sixteenth notes]	*im* or *mi* *ma* or *am* *ia* or *ai*
Chromatic	Beginning on D			

Diatonic Scales

E Major (2 octaves)

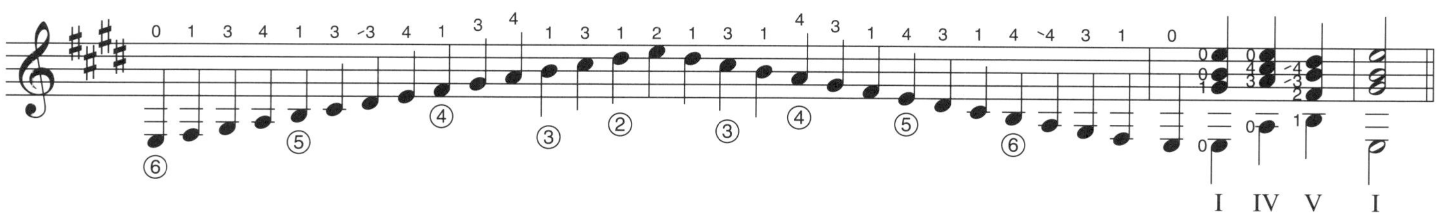

C♯ Minor Harmonic (2 octaves)

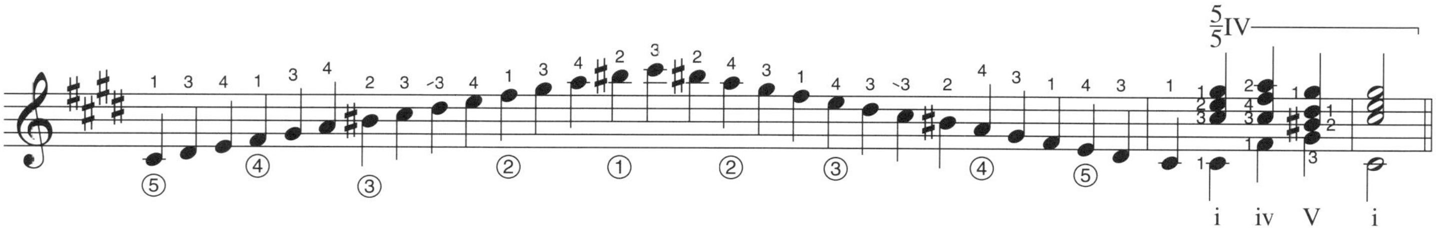

C♯ Minor Melodic (2 octaves)

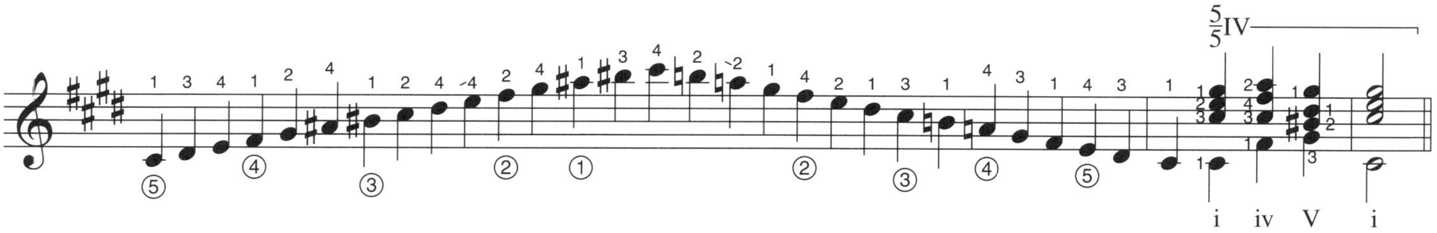

B Major (2 octaves)

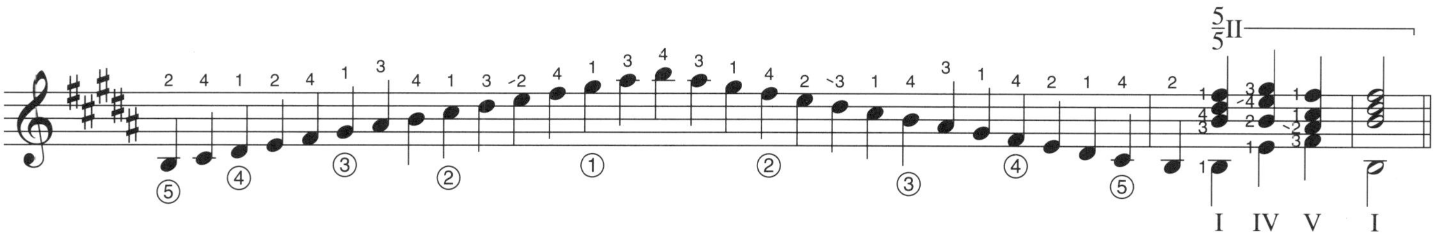

G♯ Minor Harmonic (2 octaves)

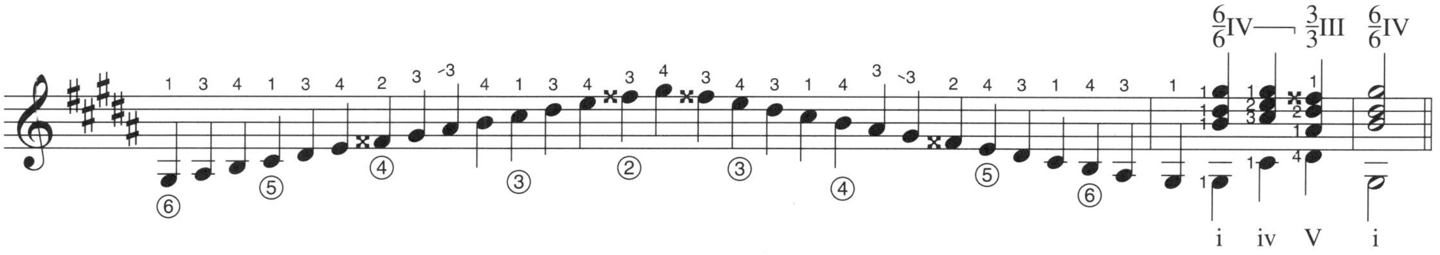

G♯ Minor Melodic (2 octaves)

F♯ Major (2 octaves)

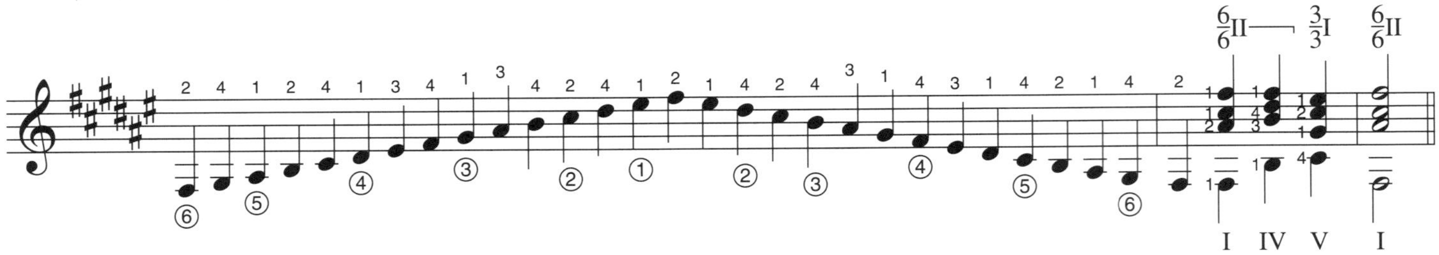

D♯ Minor Harmonic (2 octaves)

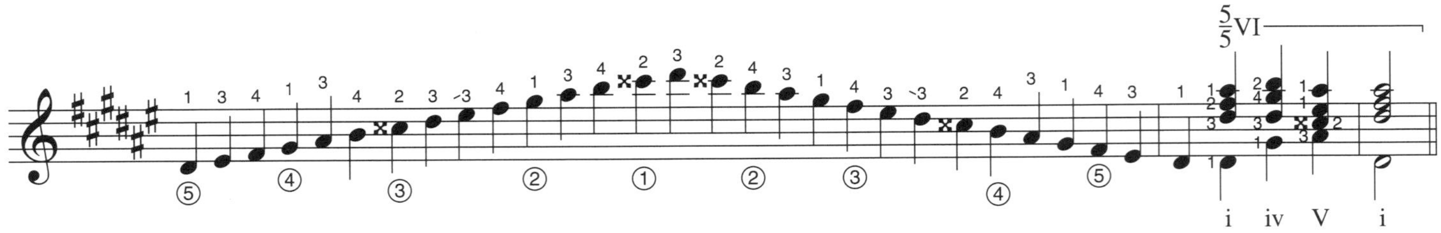

D♯ Minor Melodic (2 octaves)

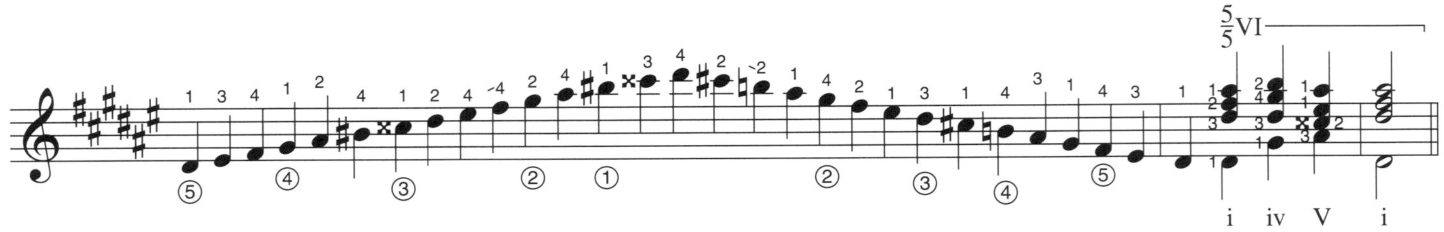

F Major (2 octaves)

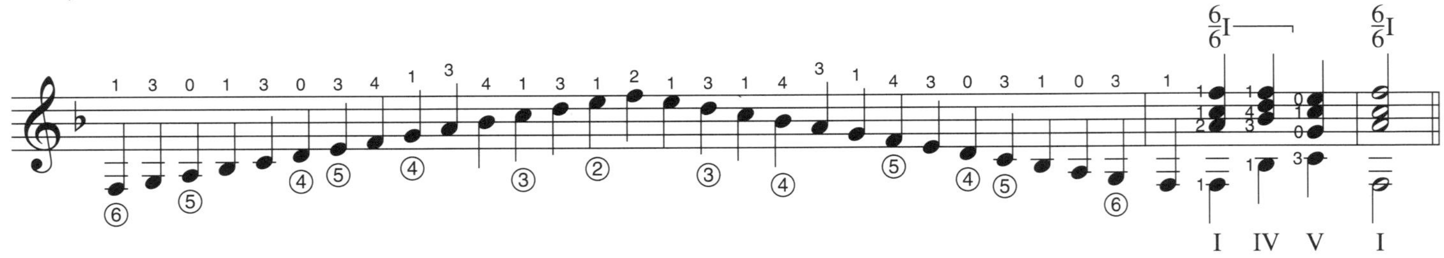

D Minor Harmonic (2 octaves)

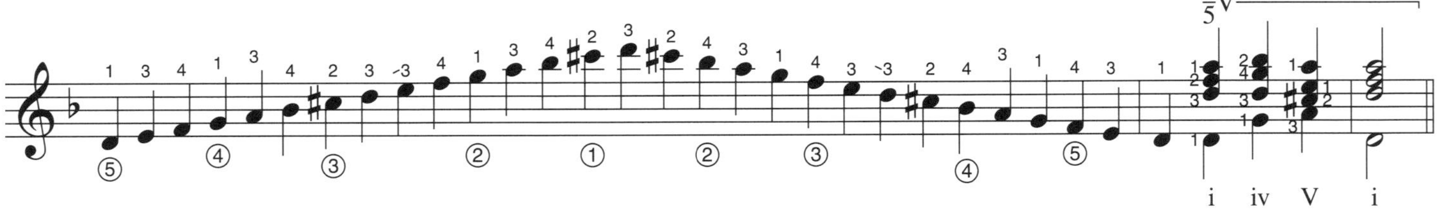

D Minor Melodic (2 octaves)

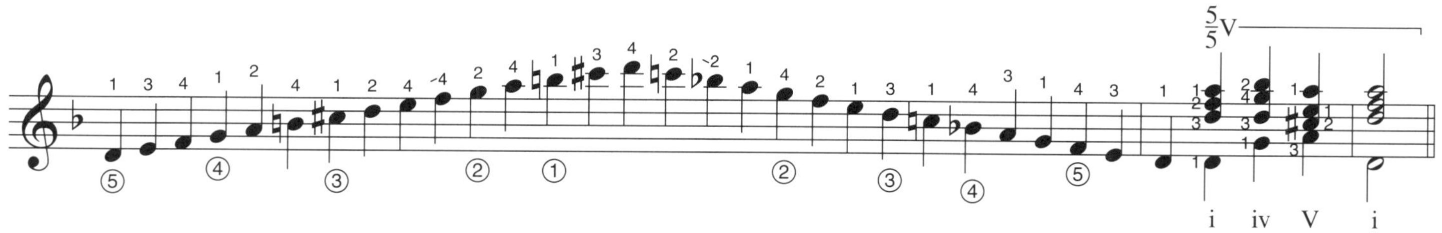

B♭ Major (2 octaves)

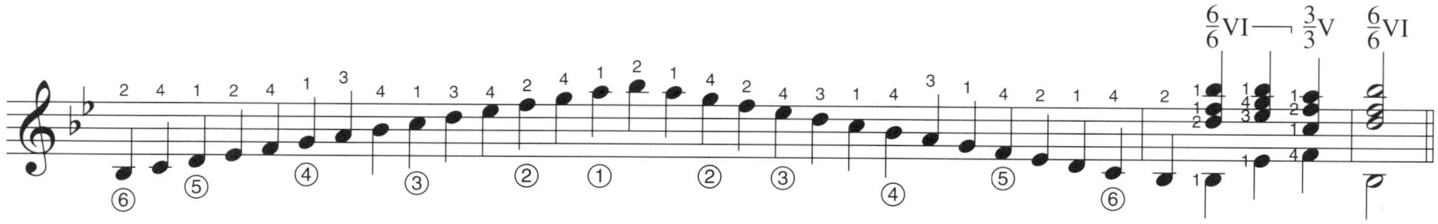

G Minor Harmonic (2 octaves)

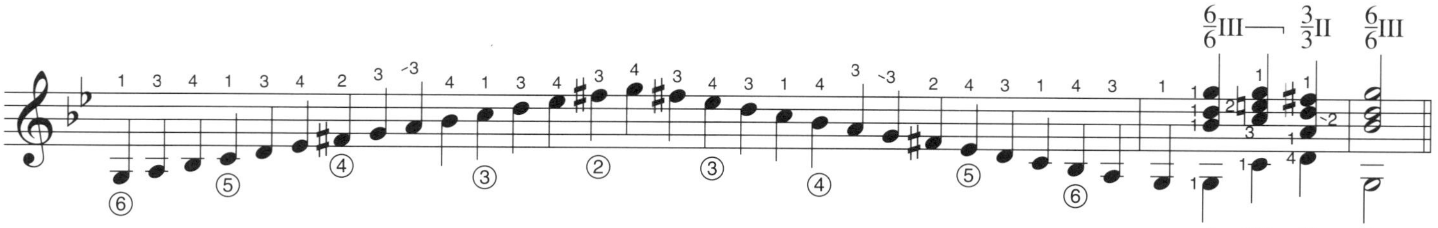

G Minor Melodic (2 octaves)

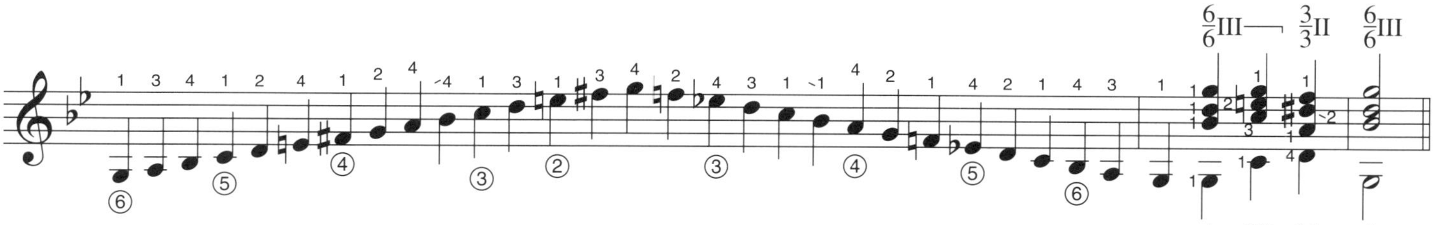

Chromatic Scale

Beginning on D (2 octaves)

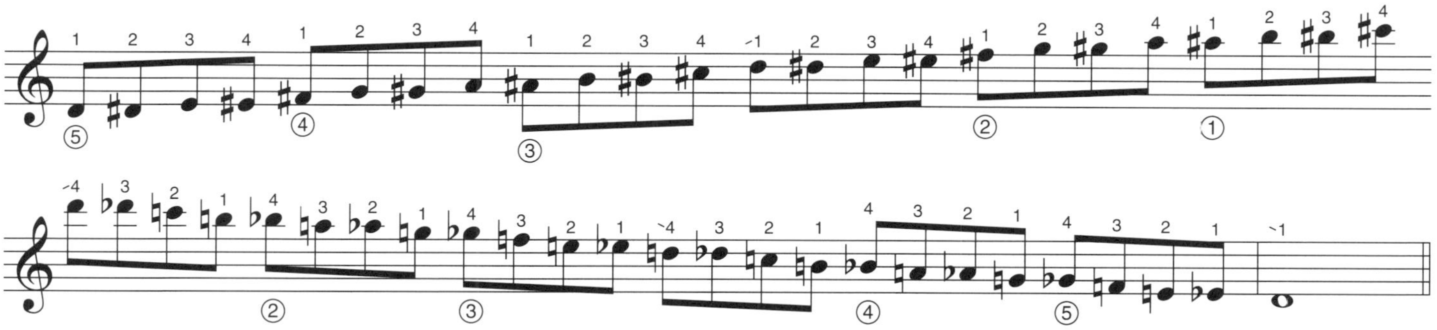

Tremolando Scales

Play all the single-note diatonic scales illustrated above in tremolando, with both rest stroke and free stroke, at or beyond the tempo given in the chart. Follow the left-hand fingering precisely and finish each scale with the given cadence. Play each scale with the note values and the right-hand fingering listed in the chart. See "Accent and Fingering Patterns" on p. 5.

Keys	Tempo	Note Values	RH Fingering
E, B, F♯, F, B♭ major C♯, G♯, D♯, D, G minor (harmonic and melodic)	♩ = 88	♪♪♪ (triplet) and ♬♬	*im* or *mi* *ma* or *am* *ia* or *ai*

Slur Scale

Play the following scales at or beyond the given tempo. Follow the left-hand fingering precisely; any right-hand fingering is acceptable.

D Major, compound triplets (1 octave)

♩ = 56

Scales in 3rds and 6ths

Play the following scales in solid (blocked) form at or beyond the given tempo. Follow the left-hand fingering precisely; any right-hand fingering is acceptable.

C Major in 3rds (1 octave)

♩ = 69

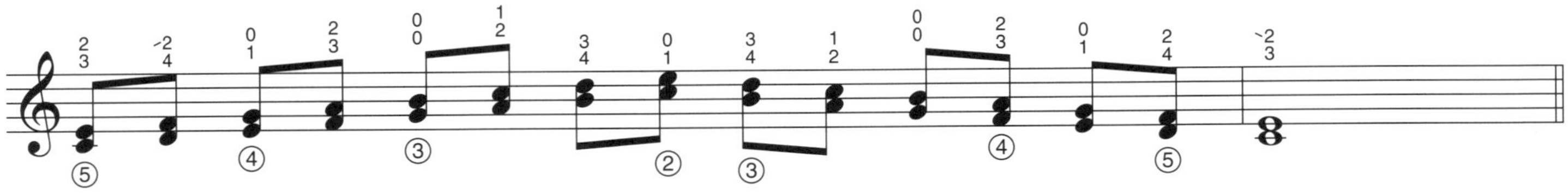

A Minor Harmonic in 3rds (1 octave)

♩ = 69

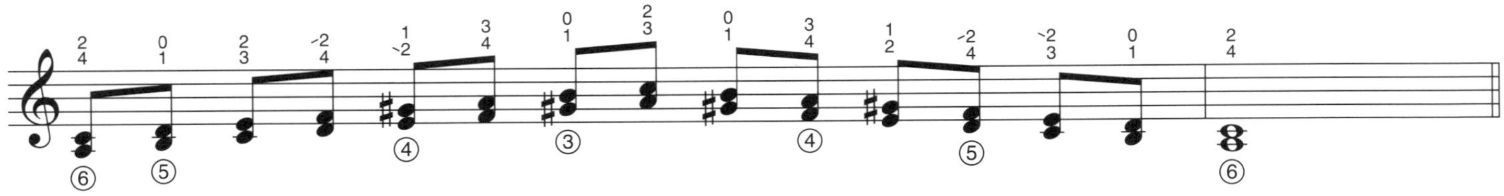

C Major in 6ths (1 octave)

♩ = 69

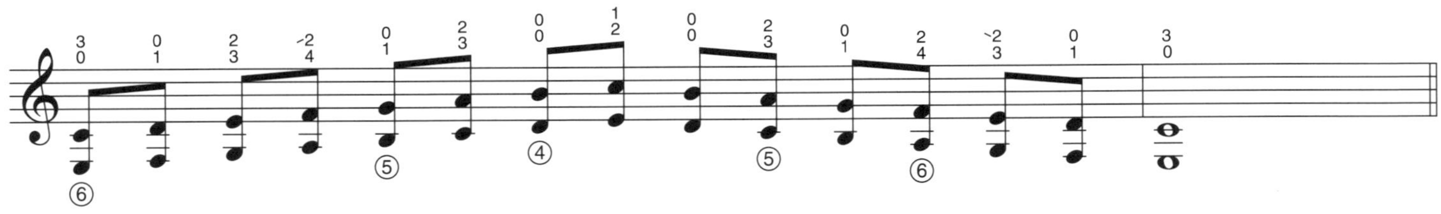

A Minor Harmonic in 6ths (1 octave)

♩ = 69

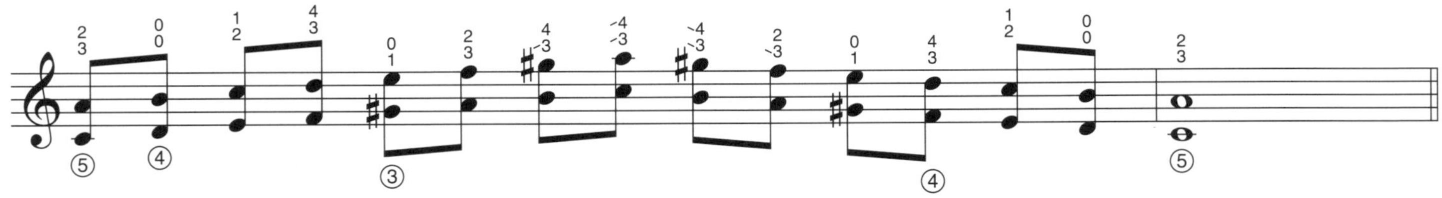

Arpeggio Patterns

Play the following arpeggio patterns at or beyond the given tempo. Use the given fingering and observe the repeat signs.

1. *p–i–m–i* and *p–i–a–m* pattern

♩ = 88

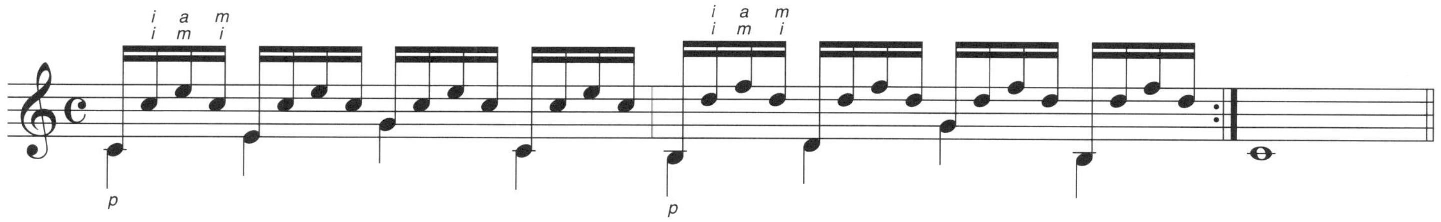

2. *p–m–i–m* and *p–a–i–m* pattern

♩ = 88

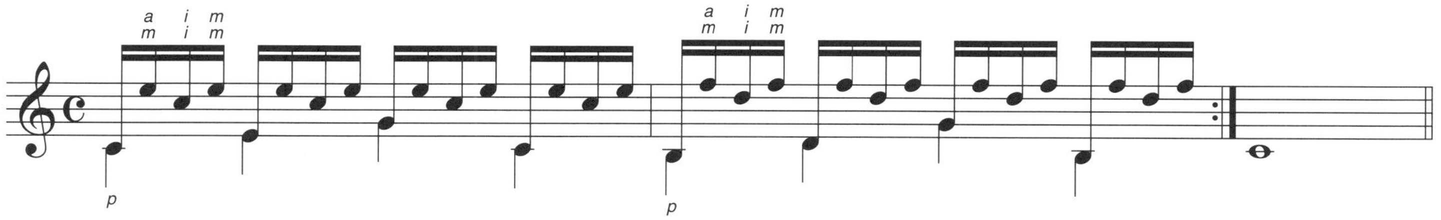

3. ascending and descending sextuplet pattern

♩ = 56

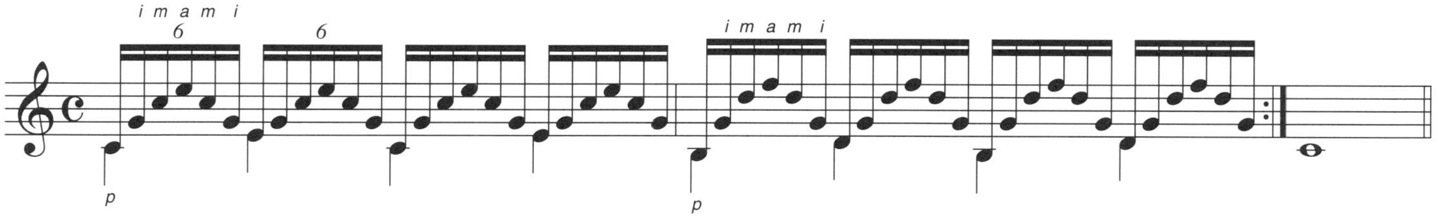

4. descending and ascending sextuplet pattern

♩ = 56

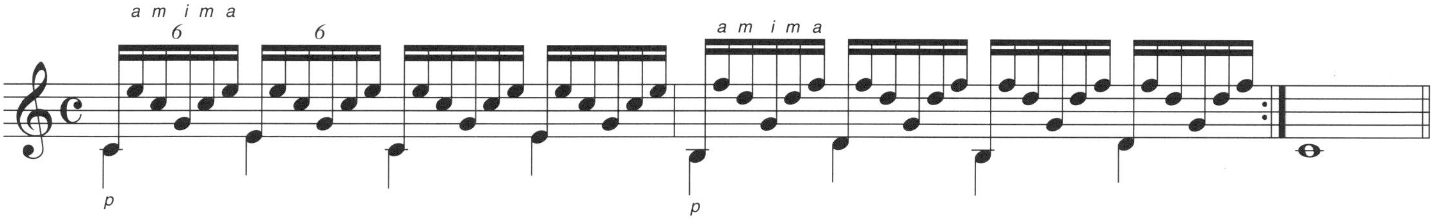

5. *p–a–m–i* tremolo pattern

♩ = 88

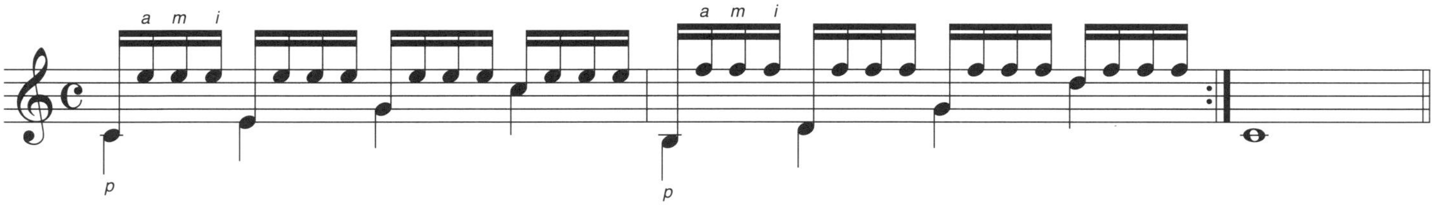

6. *p–i–m–i–p–i* pattern

♩ = 56

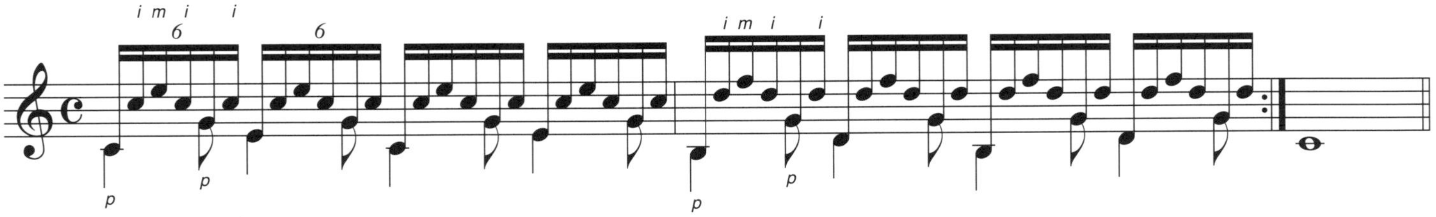

7. *p–m–i–m–p–i* pattern

♩ = 56

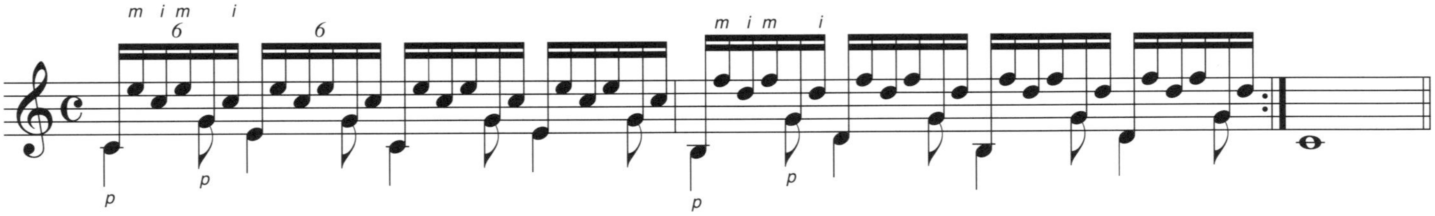

8. *p–a* dyad–*m–i* triplet pattern

♩ = 84

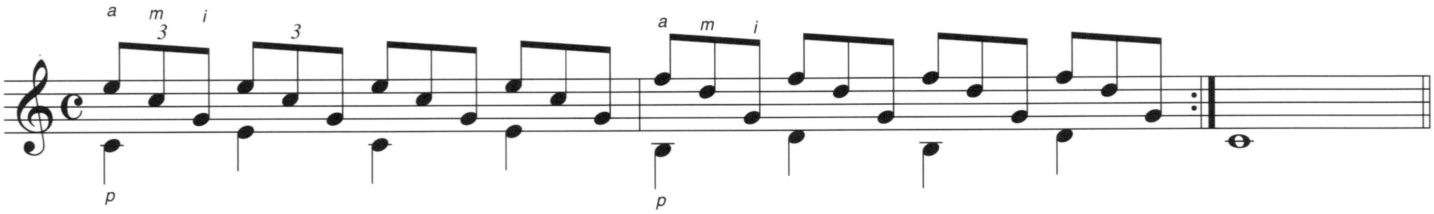

9. *p–i* dyad–*m–a* triplet pattern

♩ = 84

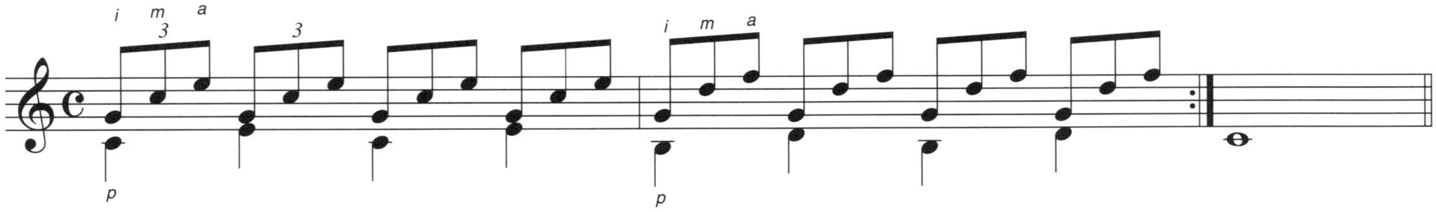

10. *p–m* dyad–*i–a* triplet pattern

♩ = 84

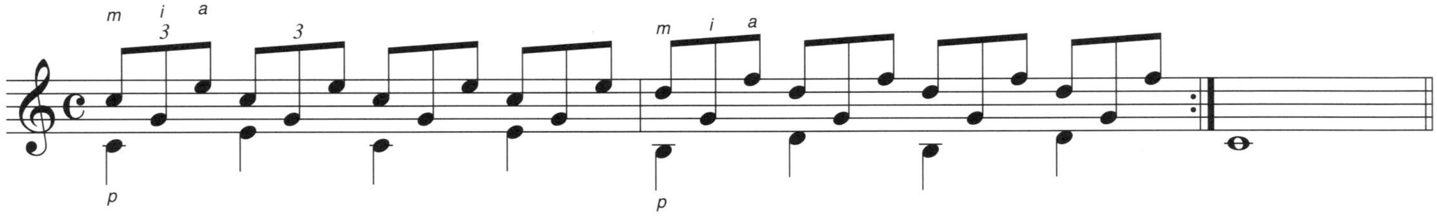

11. *p–i* dyad–*a–m* triplet pattern

♩ = 84

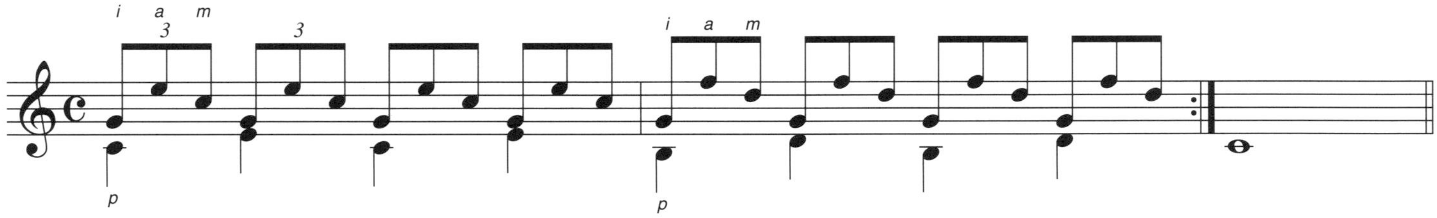

Level 7

Diatonic and Chromatic Scales

Play the following scales, in both rest stroke and free stroke, at or beyond the tempo given in the chart. Follow the left-hand fingering precisely and finish each diatonic scale with the given cadence. Play each scale with the note values and the right-hand fingering listed in the chart. See "Accent and Fingering Patterns" on p. 5.

	Keys	Tempo	Note Values	RH Fingering
Diatonic	G, E, F, A♭, D♭ major E, C♯, D, F, B♭ minor (harmonic and melodic)	♩ = 84	 and 	*im* or *mi* *ma* or *am* *ia* or *ai*
Chromatic	Beginning on A			

Diatonic Scales

G Major (3 octaves)

E Minor Harmonic (3 octaves)

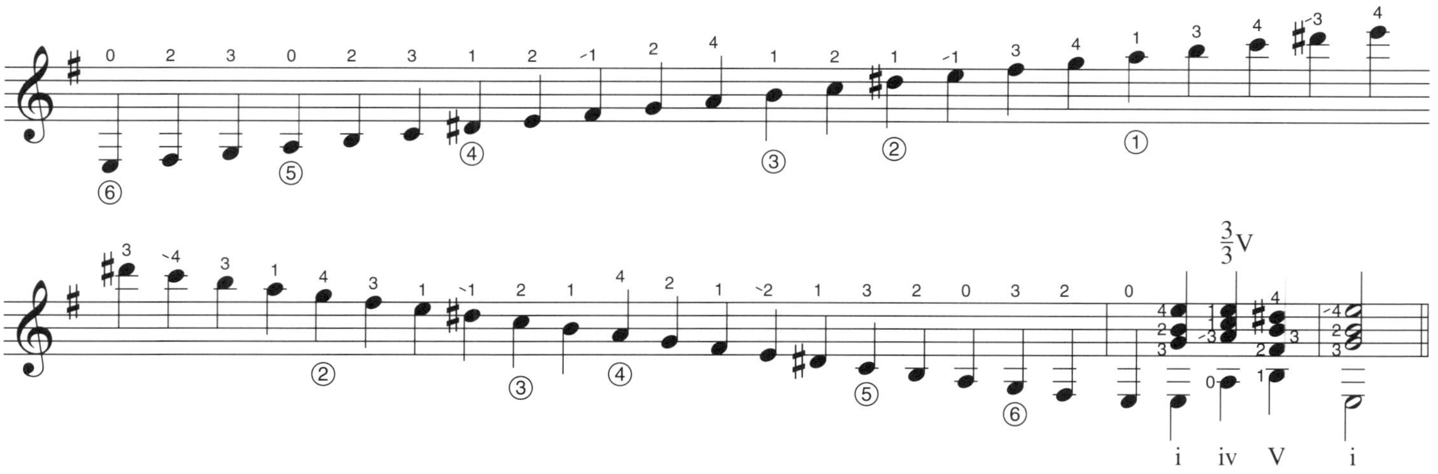

E Minor Melodic (3 octaves)

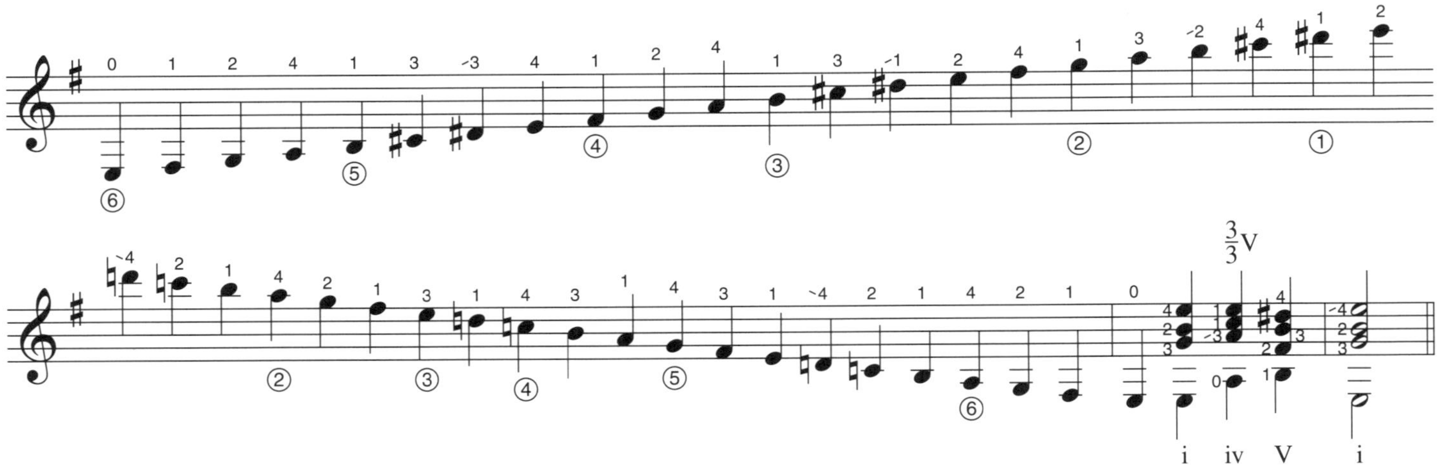

E Major (3 octaves)

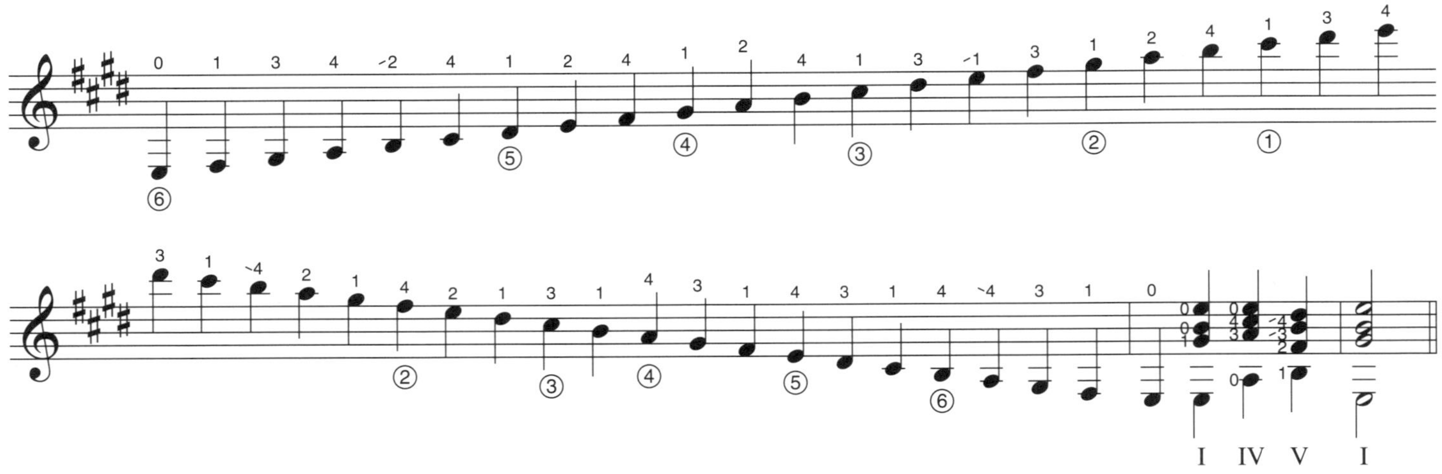

C♯ Minor Harmonic (2 octaves)

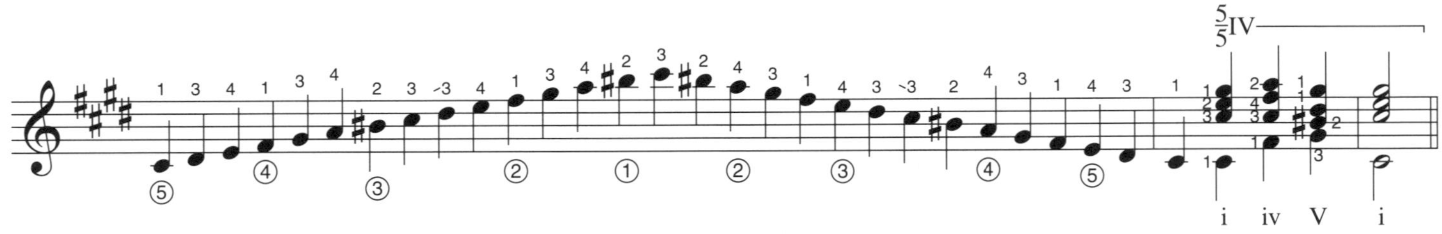

C♯ Minor Melodic (2 octaves)

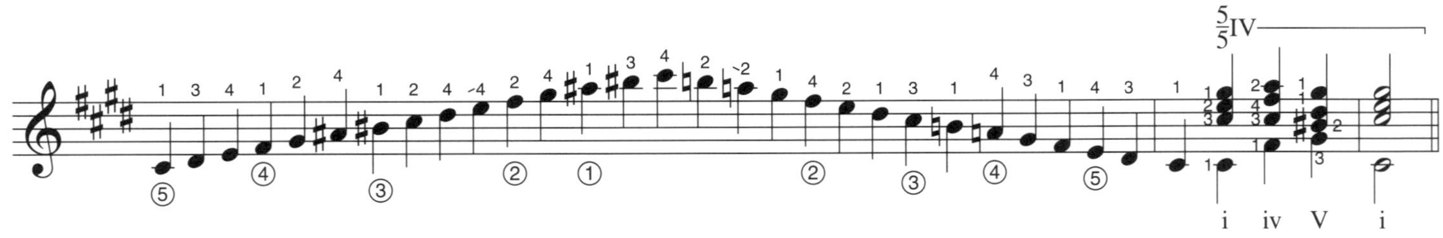

F Major (3 octaves)

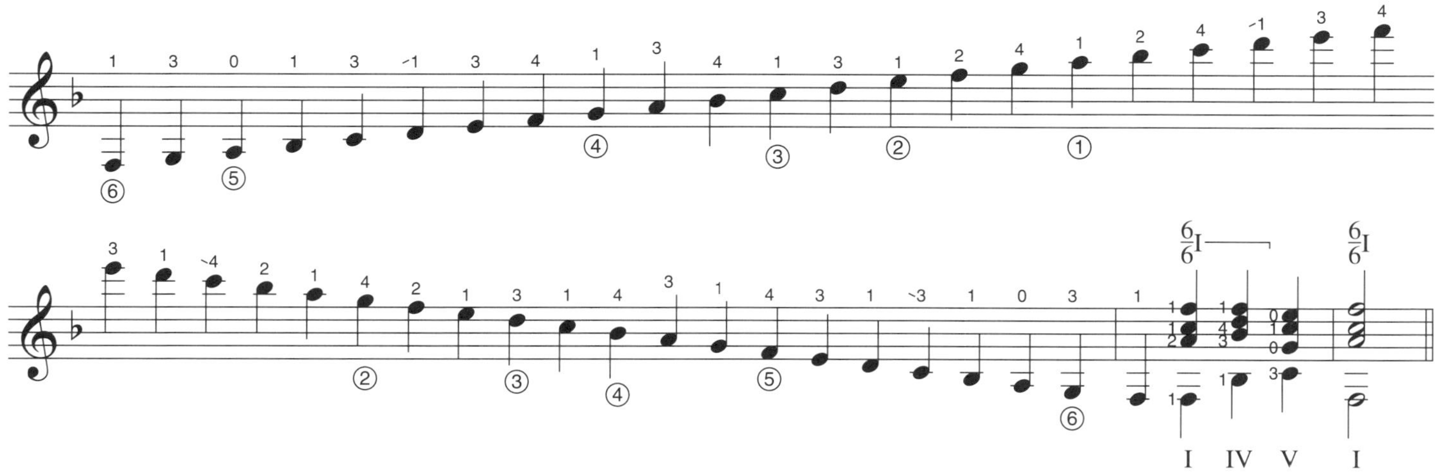

D Minor Harmonic (2 octaves)

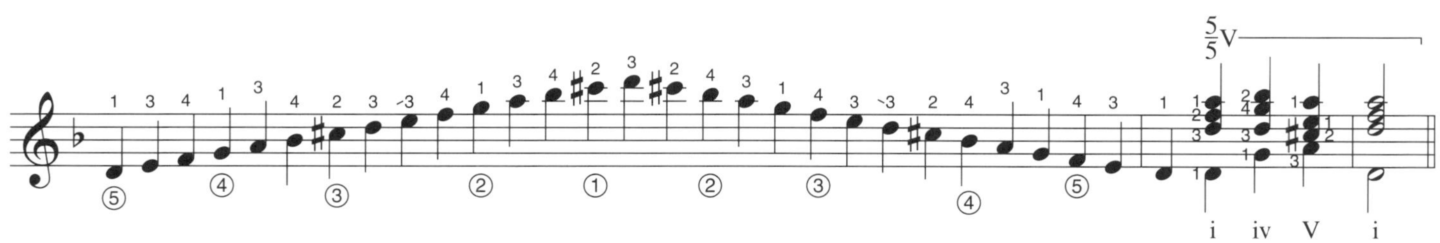

D Minor Melodic (2 octaves)

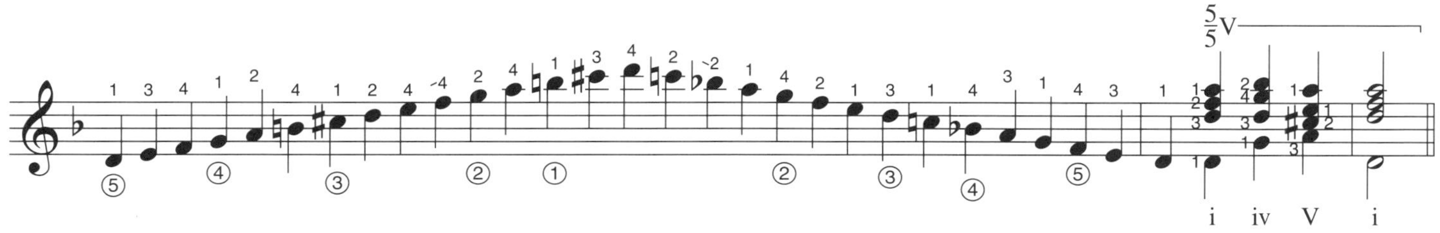

A♭ Major (2 octaves)

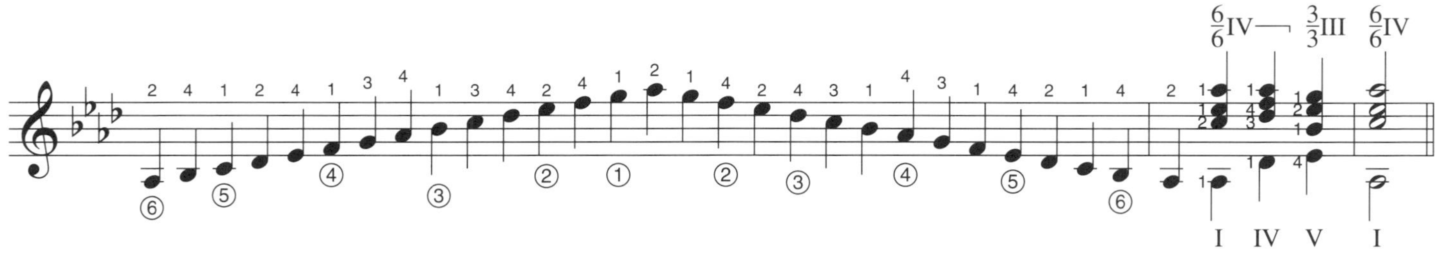

F Minor Harmonic (2 octaves)

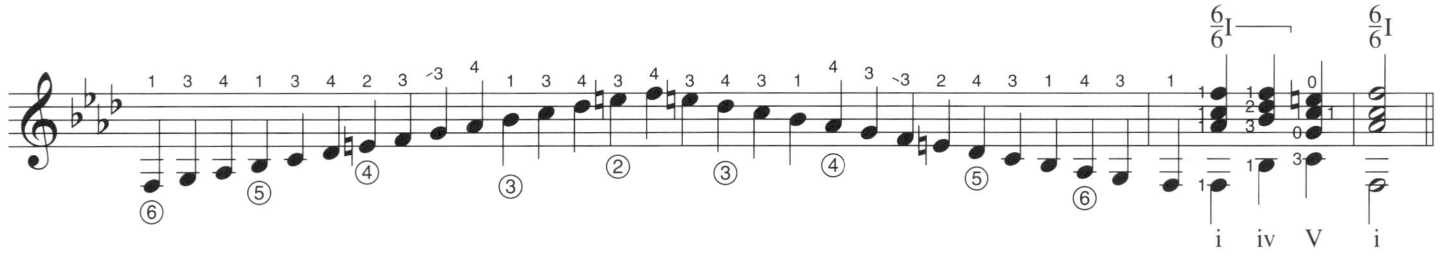

F Minor Melodic (2 octaves)

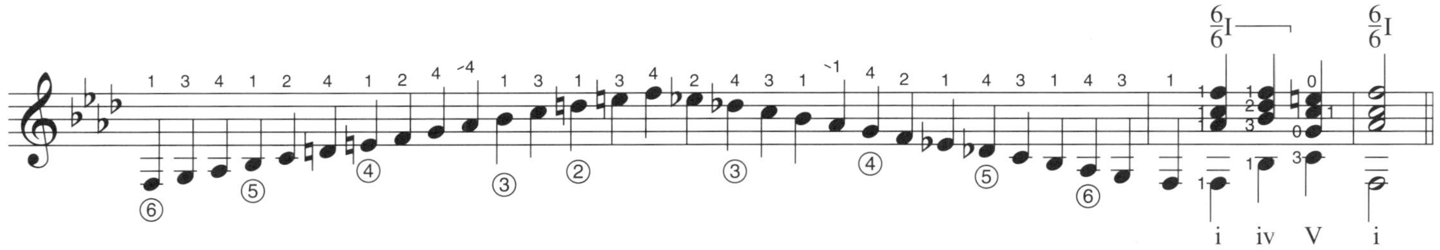

D♭ Major (2 octaves)

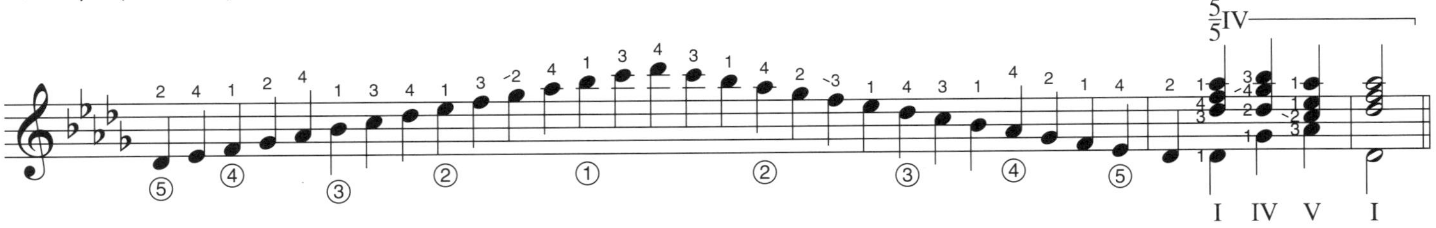

B♭ Minor Harmonic (2 octaves)

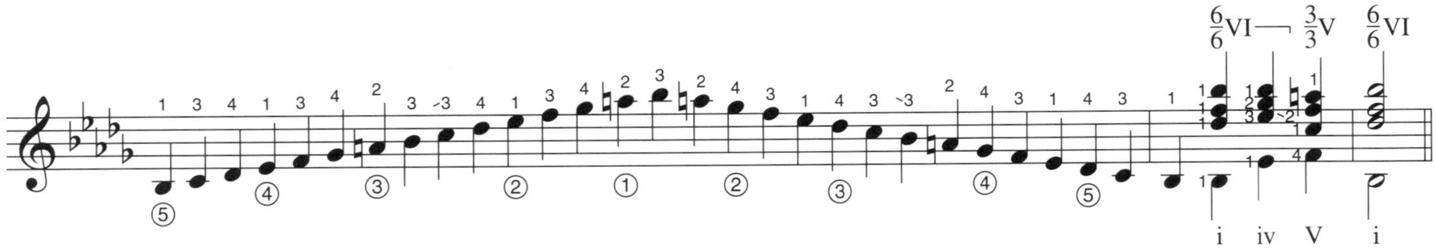

B♭ Minor Melodic (2 octaves)

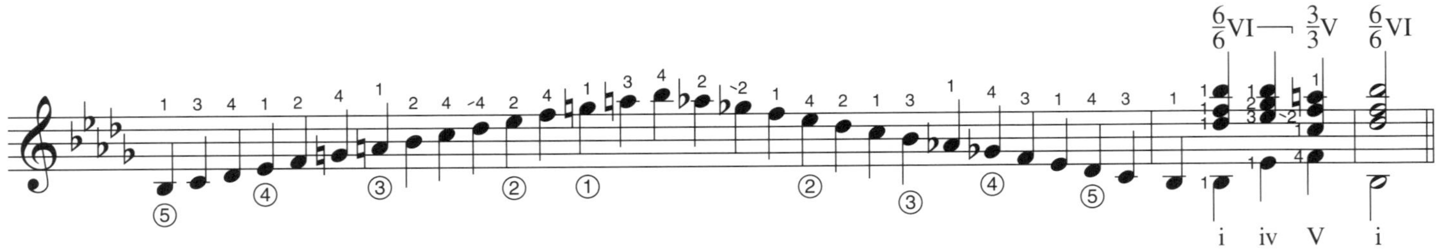

Chromatic Scale

Beginning on A (3 octaves)

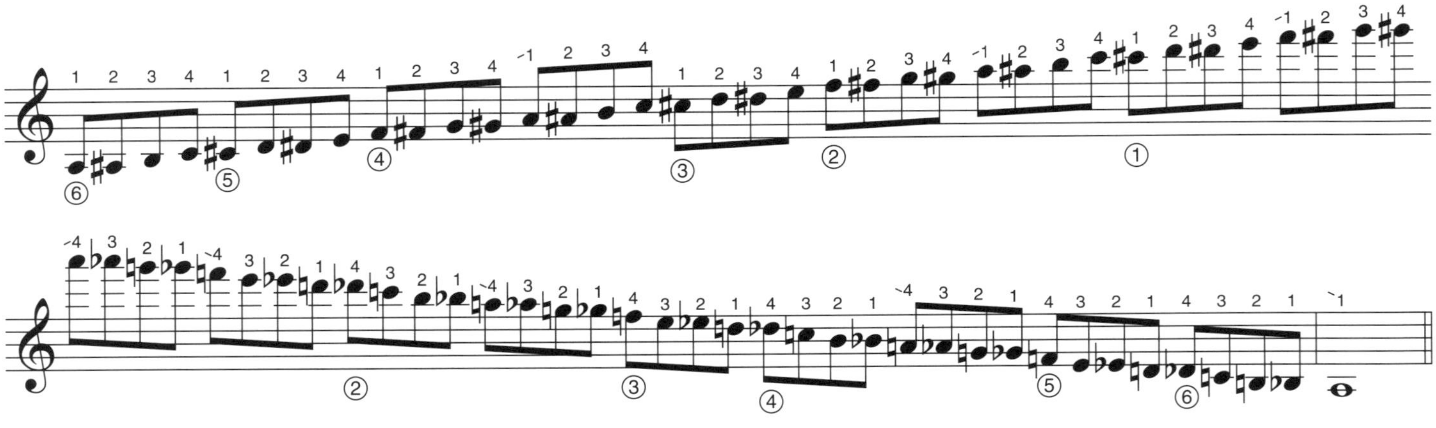

Tremolando Scales

Play the two-octave, single-note diatonic scales illustrated above in tremolando, with both rest stroke and free stroke, at or beyond the tempo given in the chart. Follow the left-hand fingering precisely and finish each scale with the given cadence. Play each scale with the note values and the right-hand fingering listed in the chart. See "Accent and Fingering Patterns" on p. 5.

Keys	Tempo	Note Values	RH Fingering
A♭, D♭ major C♯, D, F, B♭ minor (harmonic and melodic)	♩ = 96	♪♪♪ (3) and ♬♬	*im* or *mi* *ma* or *am* *ia* or *ai*

Slur Scale

Play the following scale at or beyond the given tempo. Follow the left-hand fingering precisely; any right-hand fingering is acceptable.

G Major, compound triplets (1 octave)

♩ = 80

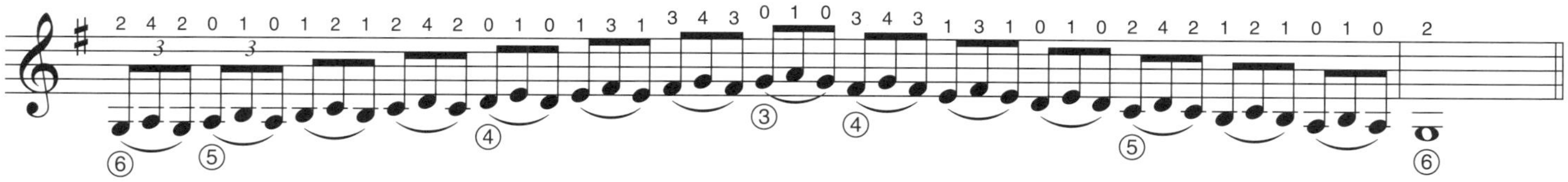

Scales in 3rds and 6ths

Play the following scales in solid (blocked) form at or beyond the given tempo. Follow the left-hand fingering precisely; any right-hand fingering is acceptable.

G Major in 3rds (1 octave)

♩ = 80

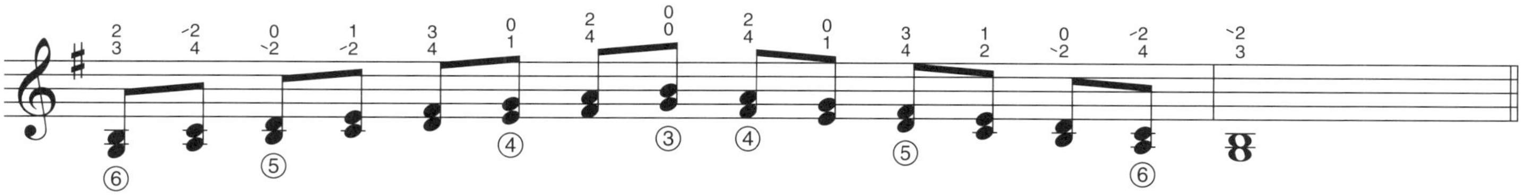

E Minor Harmonic in 3rds (1 octave)

♩ = 80

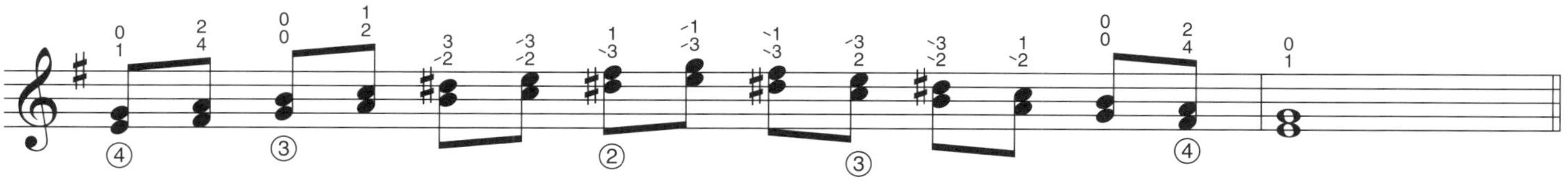

G Major in 6ths (1 octave)

♩ = 80

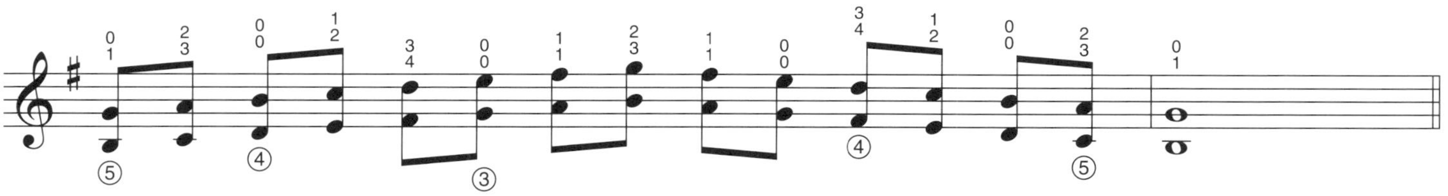

E Minor Harmonic in 6ths (1 octave)

♩ = 80

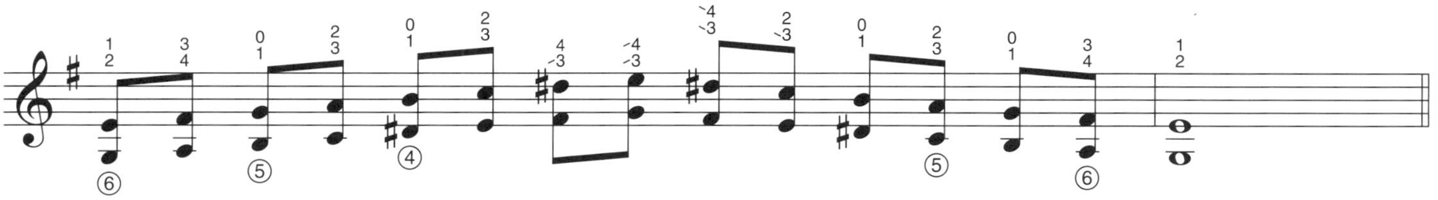

Arpeggio Patterns

Play the following arpeggio patterns at or beyond the given tempo. Use the given fingering and observe the repeat signs.

1. ascending and descending sextuplet pattern

♩ = 60

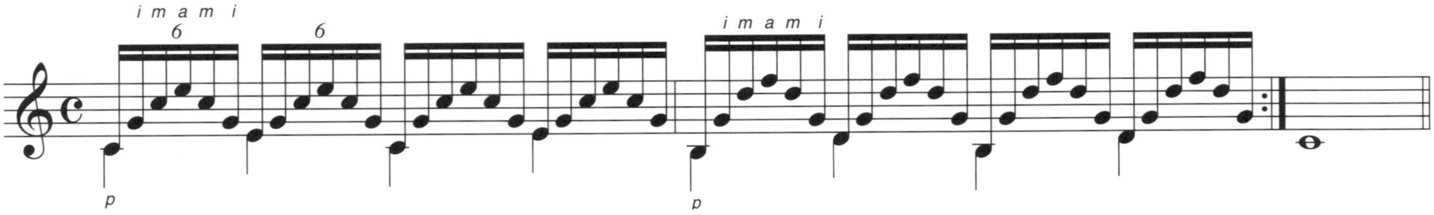

2. descending and ascending sextuplet pattern

♩ = 60

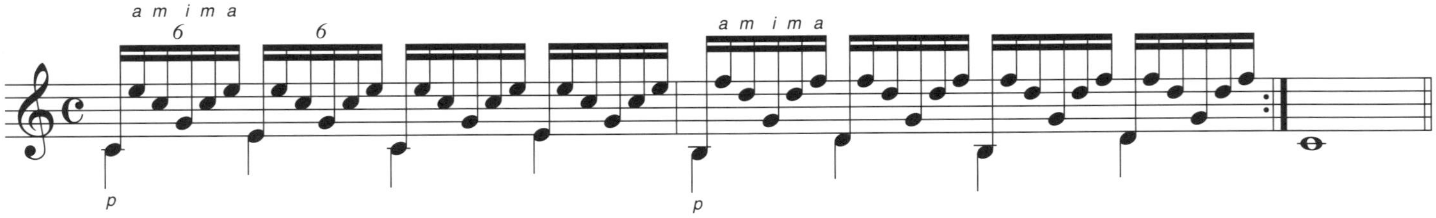

3. *p–i–m–i–p–i* pattern

♩ = 60

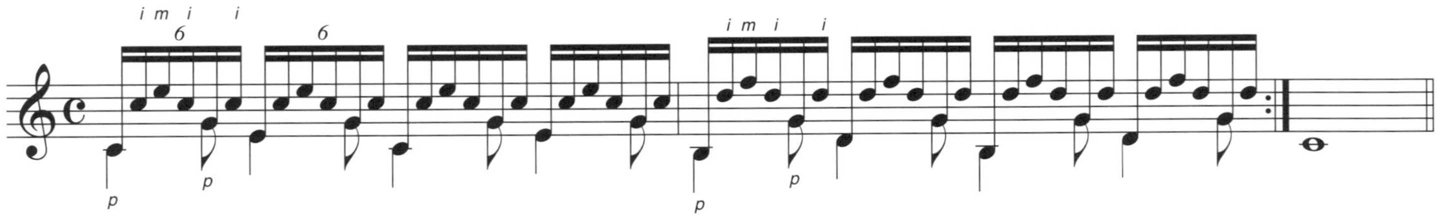

4. *p–m–i–m–p–i* pattern

♩ = 60

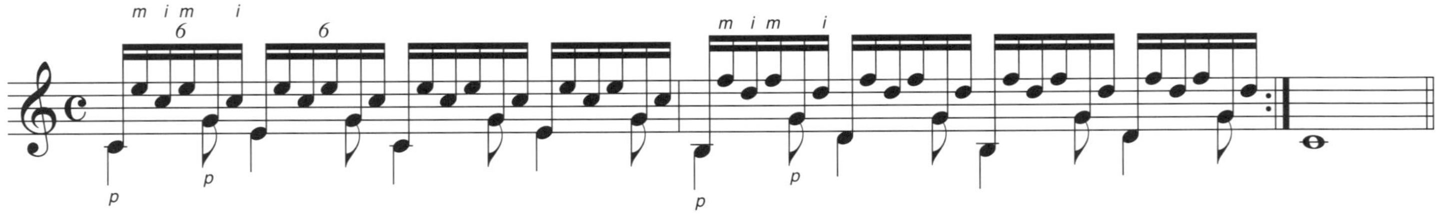

5. *p–a–m–i* tremolo pattern

♩ = 96

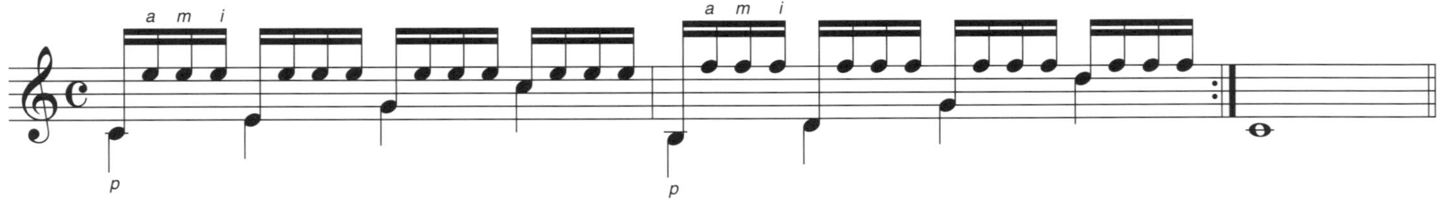

6. *p–i–m–i–a–i* alternation pattern

♩ = 60

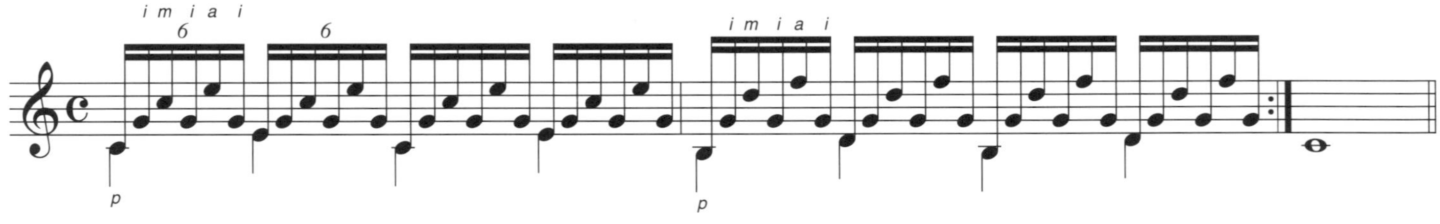

7. *p–i–a–i–m–i* alternation pattern

♩ = 60

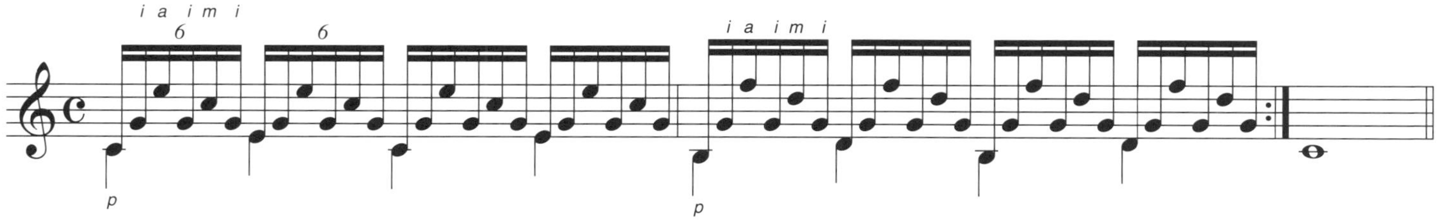

8. *p–i–m* crossing pattern

♩ = 120

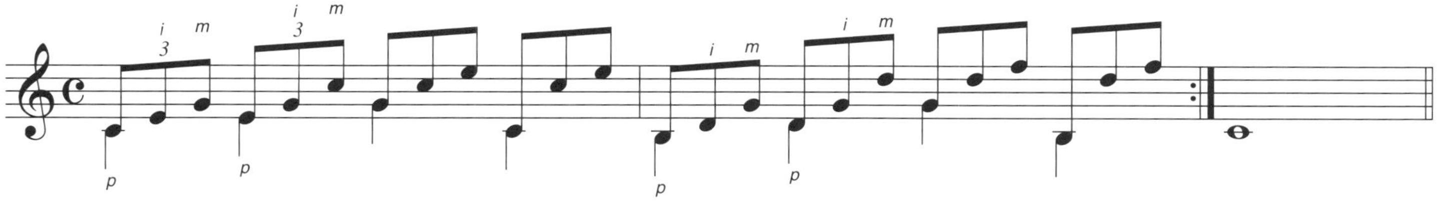

9. *m–i–p* crossing pattern

♩ = 120

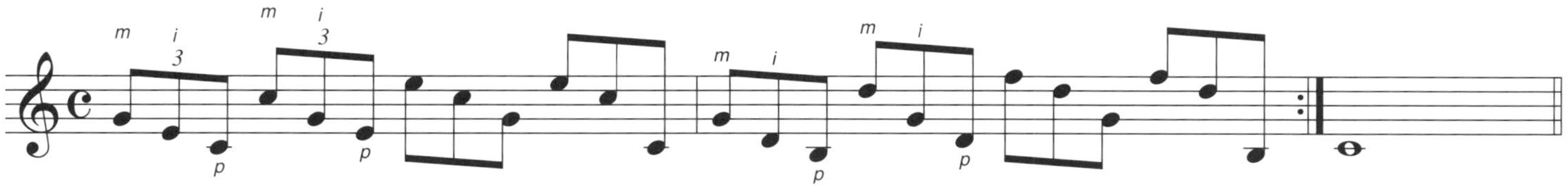

10. *p–m–i* crossing pattern

♩ = 120

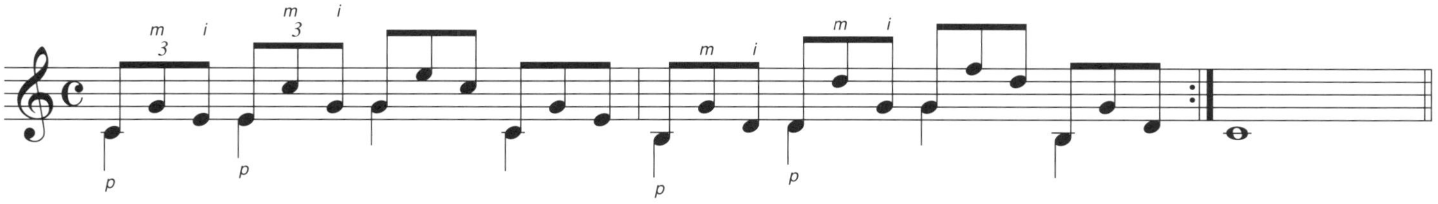

11. *p–a* dyad–*i–m–i* pattern

♩ = 84

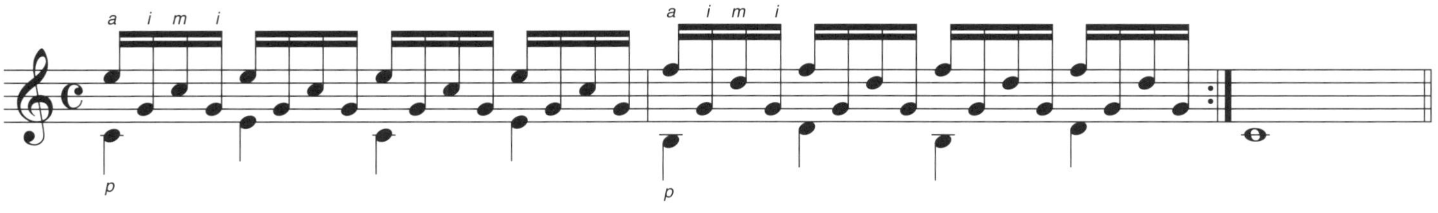

12. *p–a* dyad–*m–i–m* pattern

♩ = 84

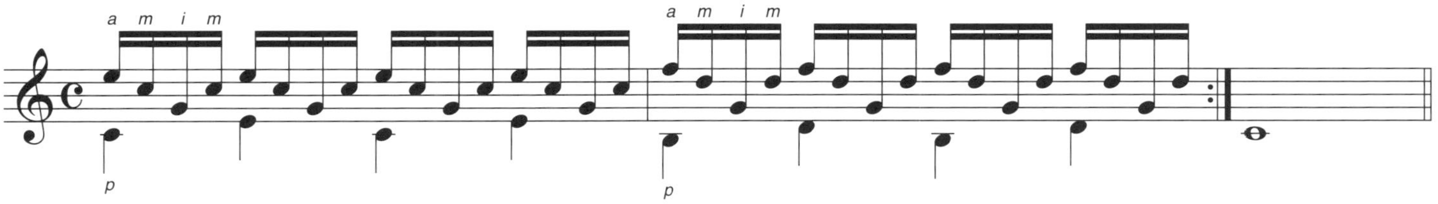

Level 8

Diatonic and Chromatic Scales

Play the following scales, in both rest stroke and free stroke, at or beyond the tempo given in the chart. Any logical left-hand fingering is acceptable. Finish each diatonic scale with the given cadence. Play each scale with the note values and the right-hand fingering listed in the chart. See "Accent and Fingering Patterns" on p. 5.

	Keys	Tempo	Note Values	RH Fingering
Diatonic	E, B, F, B♭, A♭ major C♯, G♯, D, G, F minor (harmonic and melodic)	♩ = 96	3 ♪♪♪ and ♬♬	*im* or *mi* *ia* or *ai*
Chromatic	Beginning on A♯	♩ = 88		*ma* or *am*

Diatonic Scales

E Major (2 octaves)

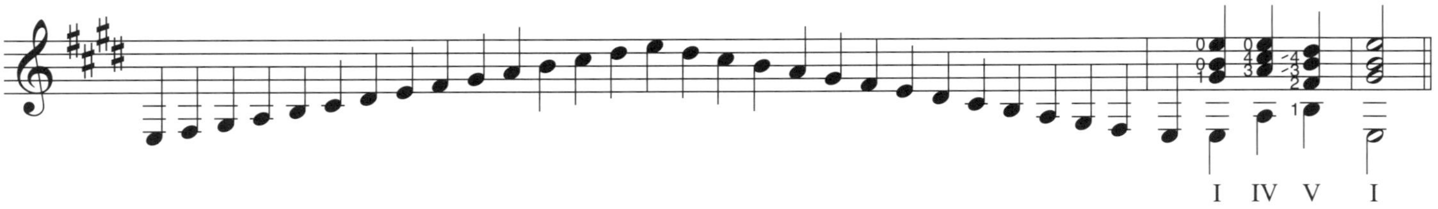

C♯ Minor Harmonic (2 octaves)

C♯ Minor Melodic (2 octaves)

B Major (2 octaves)

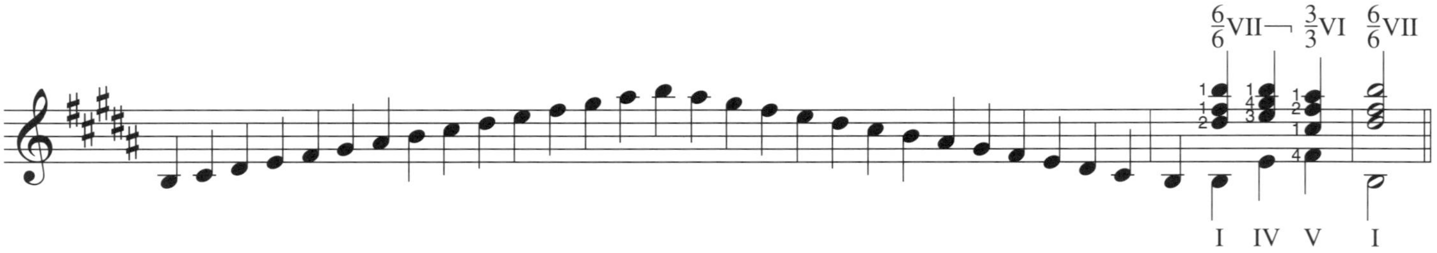

G♯ Minor Harmonic (2 octaves)

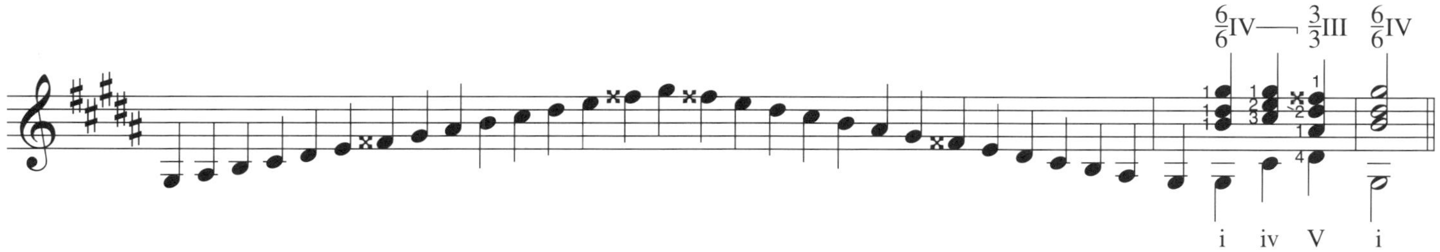

G♯ Minor Melodic (2 octaves)

F Major (3 octaves)

D Minor Harmonic (2 octaves)

D Minor Melodic (2 octaves)

B♭ Major (3 octaves)

G Minor Harmonic (3 octaves)

G Minor Melodic (3 octaves)

A♭ Major (3 octaves)

F Minor Harmonic (3 octaves)

F Minor Melodic (3 octaves)

Chromatic Scale
Beginning on A♯ (3 octaves)

Tremolando Scales

Play the two-octave, single-note diatonic scales illustrated above in tremolando, with both rest stroke and free stroke, at or beyond the tempo given in the chart. Any logical left-hand fingering is acceptable. Finish each scale with the given cadence. Play each scale with the note values and the right-hand fingering listed in the chart. See "Accent and Fingering Patterns" on p. 5.

Keys	Tempo	Note Values	RH Fingering
E, B major C♯, G♯, D minor (harmonic and melodic)	♩ = 108 ♩ = 100		*im* or *mi* *ia* or *ai* *ma* or *am*

Slur Scales

Play the following scales at or beyond the given tempo. Any logical left-hand fingering is acceptable. The printed left-hand fingering is given as a suggestion.

C Major, compound triplets (1 octave)

♩ = 100

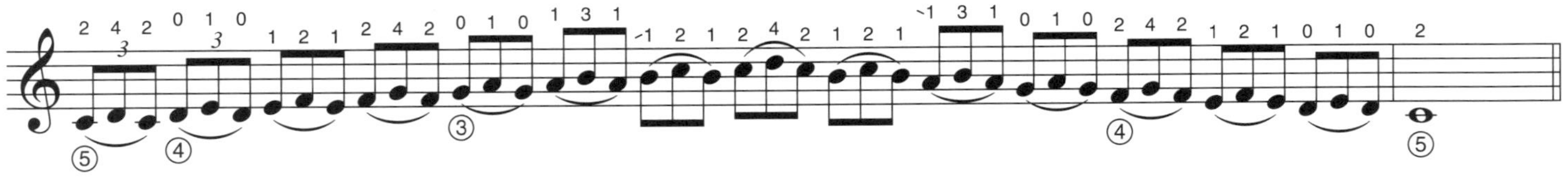

A Major, compound triplets (1 octave)

♩ = 100

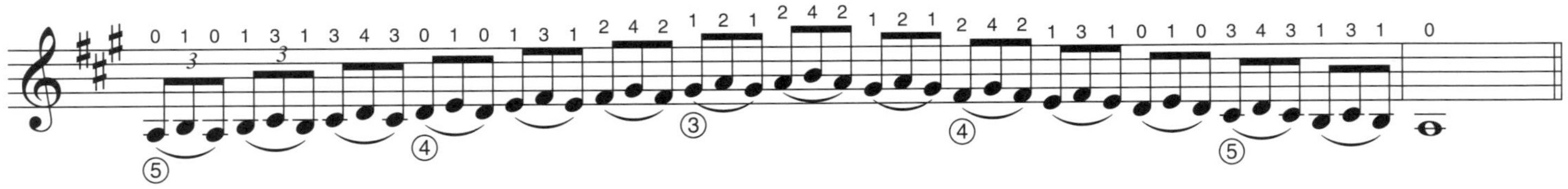

Scales in 3rds and 6ths

Play the following scales in solid (blocked) form at or beyond the given tempo. Any logical left-hand fingering is acceptable. The printed left-hand fingering is given as a suggestion.

F Major in 3rds (2 octaves)

♩ = 88

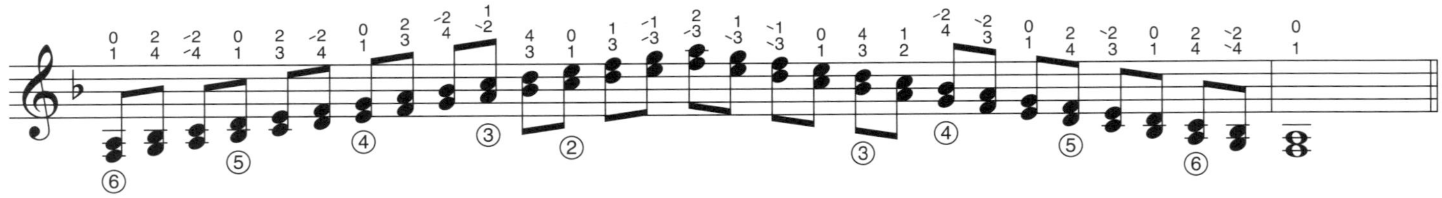

D Minor Harmonic in 3rds (2 octaves)

♩ = 88

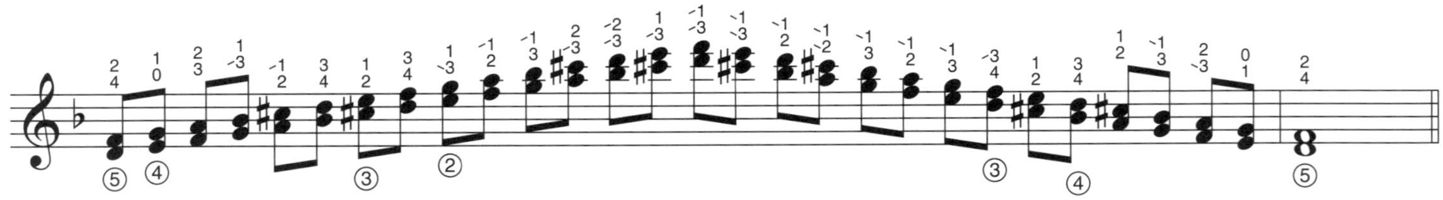

F Major in 6ths (2 octaves)

♩ = 88

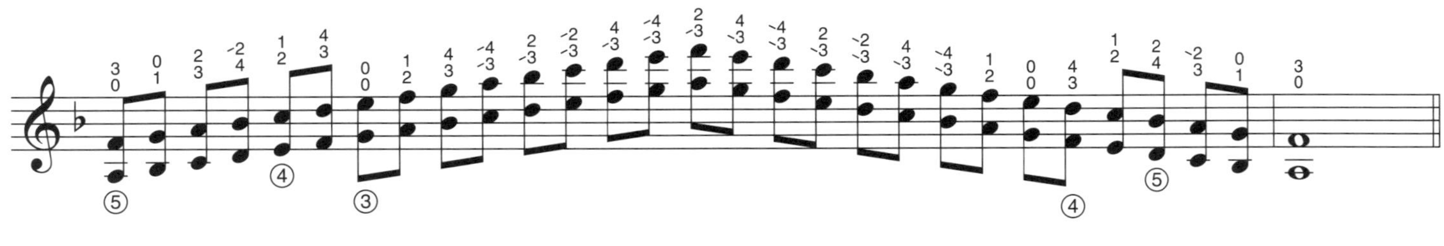

D Minor Harmonic in 6ths (2 octaves)

♩ = 88

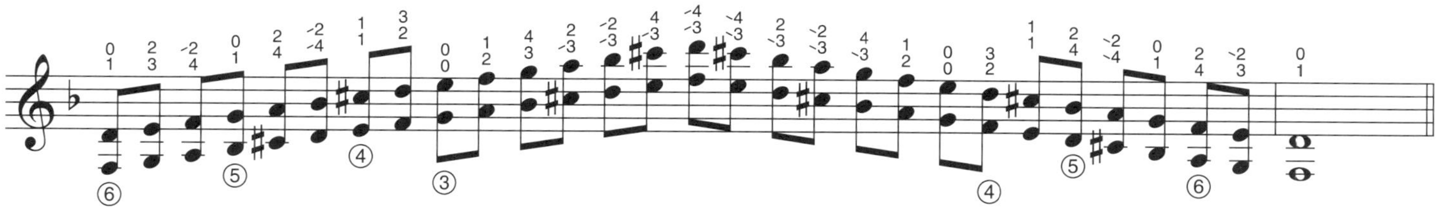

Arpeggio Patterns

Play the following arpeggio patterns at or beyond the given tempo. Use the given fingering and observe the repeat signs.

1. *p–a–m–i* tremolo pattern

♩ = 108

2. *p–i–m–i–p–i* pattern

♩ = 66

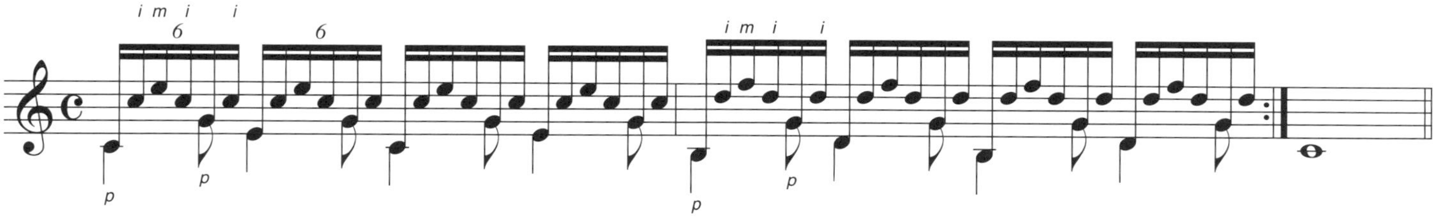

3. *p–m–i–m–p–i* pattern

♩ = 66

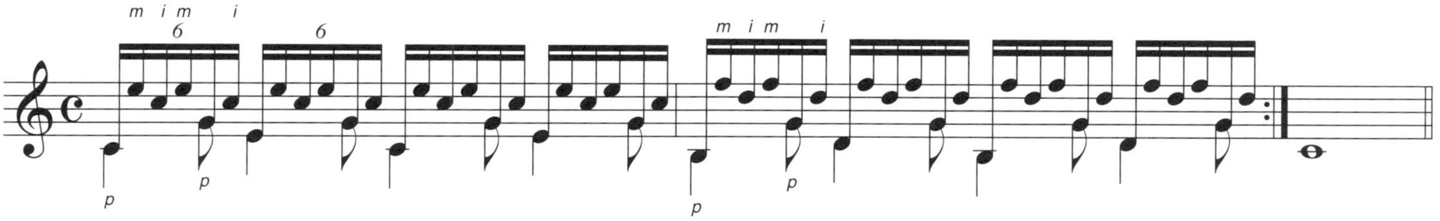

4. *p–i–m* crossing pattern

♩ = 132

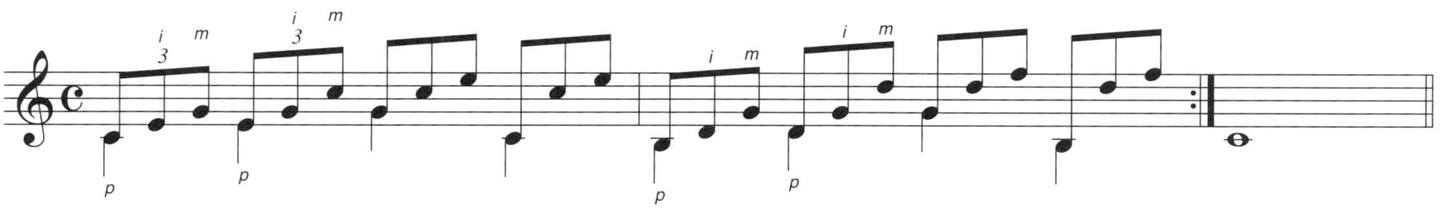

5. *m–i–p* crossing pattern

♩ = 132

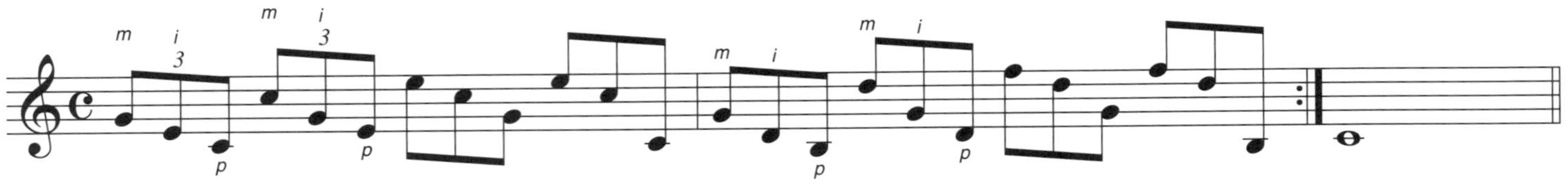

6. *p–m–i* crossing pattern

♩ = 132

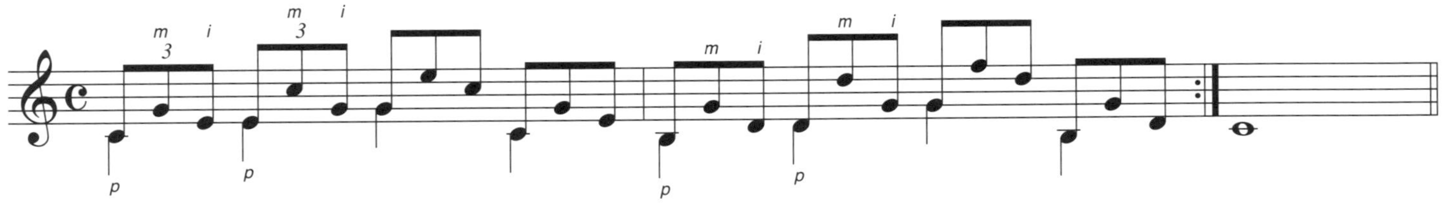

7. *p–i–m–i–a–i* alternation pattern

♩ = 66

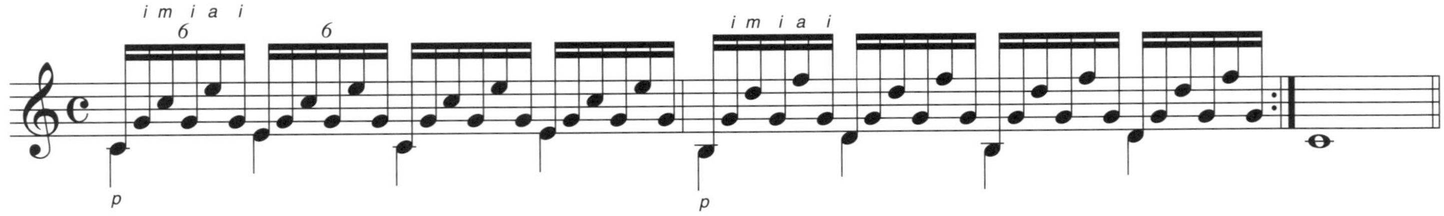

8. *p–i–a–i–m–i* alternation pattern

♩ = 66

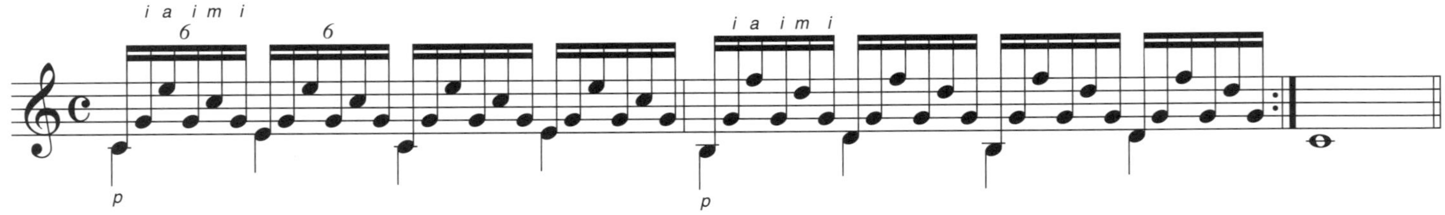

9. *p–a–m–a–m–i* sextuplet pattern

♩ = 66

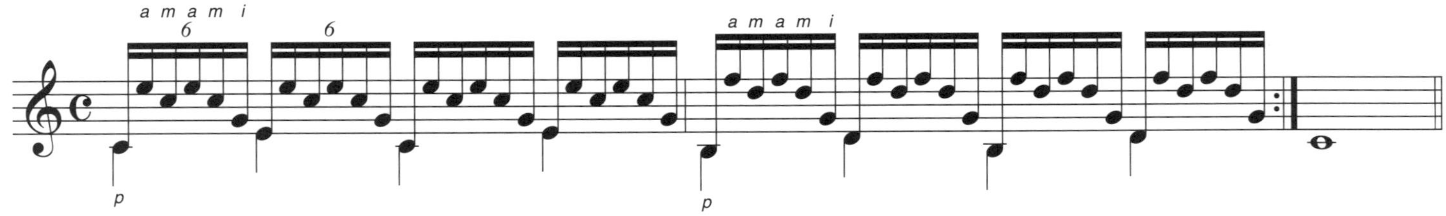

10. low–high pattern

♩ = 92

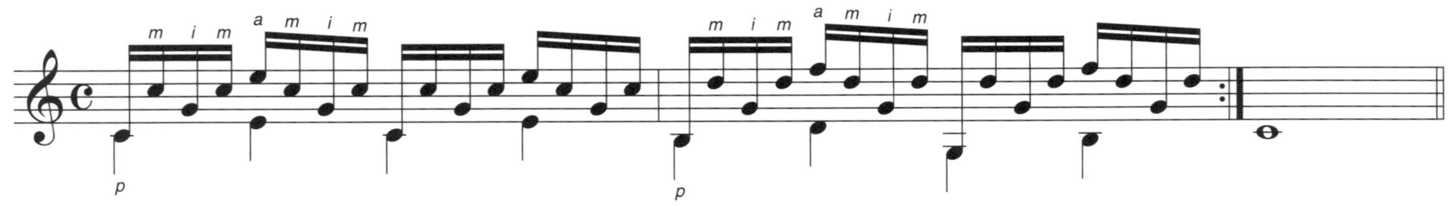

11. descending and ascending pattern

♩ = 92

12. two-phase pattern

♩ = 92

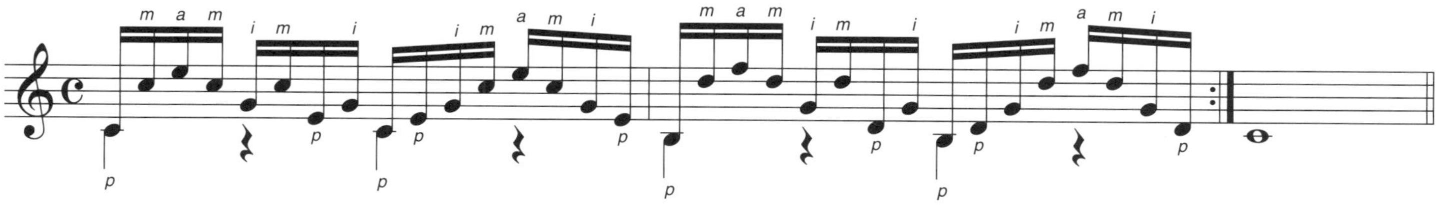

Level 9

Diatonic and Chromatic Scales

Play the following scales, in both rest stroke and free stroke, at or beyond the tempo given in the chart. Any logical left-hand fingering is acceptable. Finish each diatonic scale with the given cadence. Play each scale with the note values and the right-hand fingering listed in the chart. See "Accent and Fingering Patterns" on p. 5.

	Keys	Tempo	Note Values	RH Fingering
Diatonic	C, A, E, B, F major A, F♯, C♯, G♯ D minor (harmonic and melodic)	♩ = 108	♪♪♪ (3) and ♬♬	*im* or *mi* *ia* or *ai*
Chromatic	Beginning on B	♩ = 96		*ma* or *am*

Diatonic Scales

C Major (2 octaves)

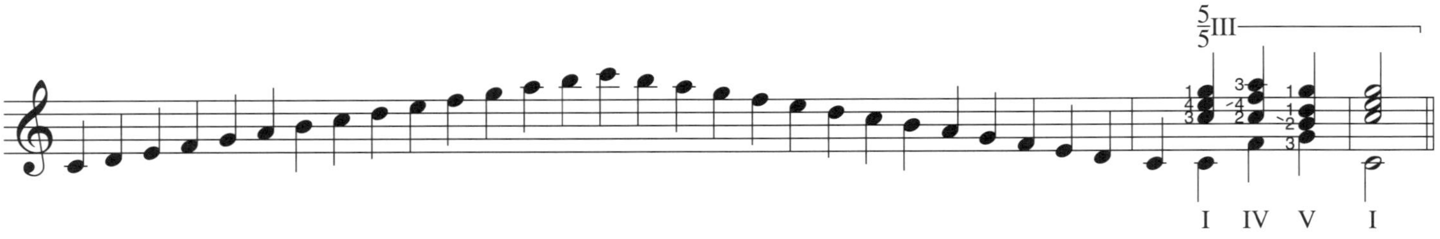

A Minor Harmonic (3 octaves)

A Minor Melodic (3 octaves)

A Major (3 octaves)

F♯ Minor Harmonic (3 octaves)

F♯ Minor Melodic (3 octaves)

E Major (3 octaves)

C♯ Minor Harmonic (2 octaves)

C♯ Minor Melodic (2 octaves)

B Major (3 octaves)

G♯ Minor Harmonic (3 octaves)

G Minor Melodic (3 octaves)

F Major (2 octaves)

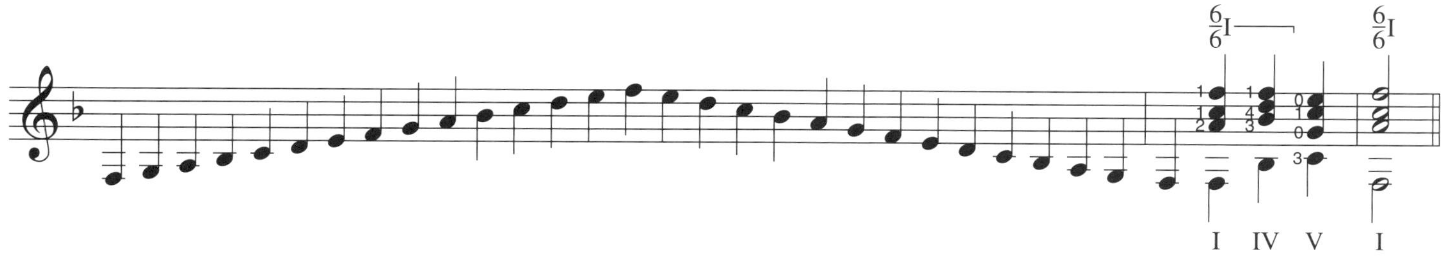

D Minor Harmonic (2 octaves)

D Minor Melodic (2 octaves)

Chromatic Scale

Beginning on B (3 octaves)

Tremolando Scales

Play the two-octave, single-note diatonic scales illustrated above in tremolando, with both rest stroke and free stroke, at or beyond the tempo given in the chart. Any logical left-hand fingering is acceptable. Finish each scale with the given cadence. Play each scale with the note values and the right-hand fingering listed in the chart. See "Accent and Fingering Patterns" on p. 5.

Keys	Tempo	Note Values	RH Fingering
C, F major C♯, D minor (harmonic and melodic)	♩ = 116 ♩ = 104	 and 	*im* or *mi* *ia* or *ai* *ma* or *am*

Slur Scales

Play the following scales at or beyond the given tempo. Any logical left-hand fingering is acceptable. The printed left-hand fingering is given as a suggestion.

G Major, compound triplets (2 octaves)

♩ = 126

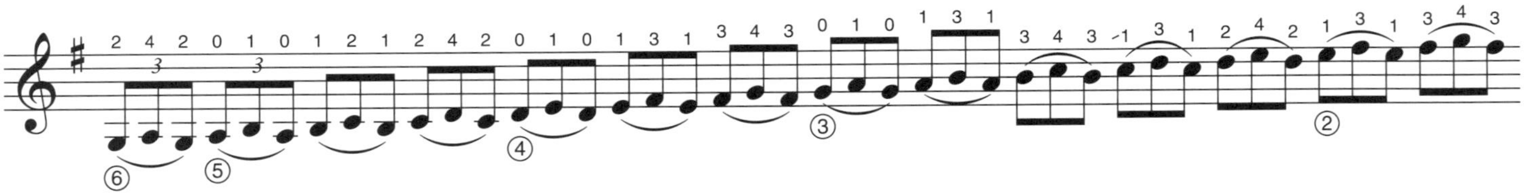

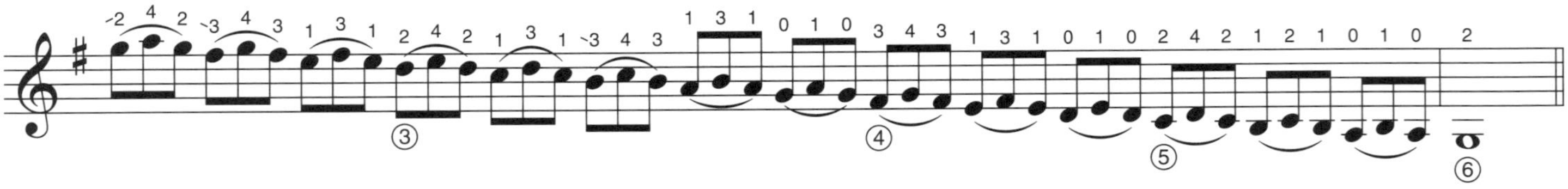

A Major, compound triplets (2 octaves)

♩ = 126

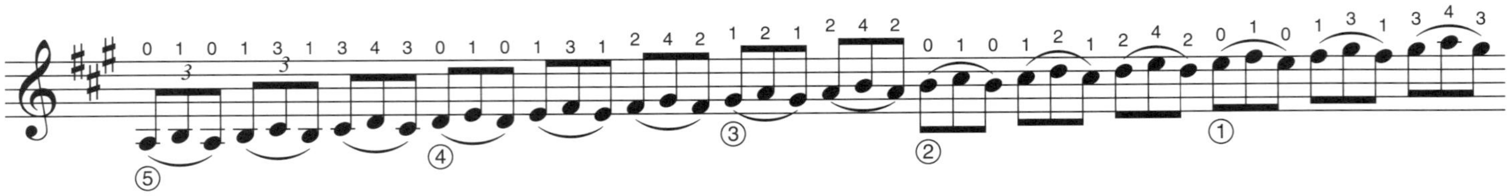

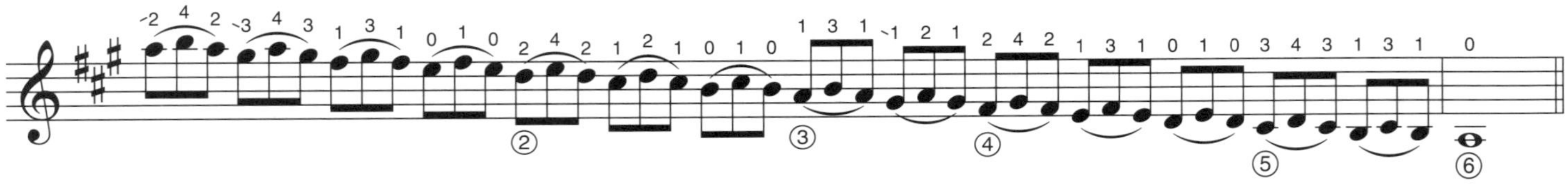

Scales in 3rds and 6ths

Play the following scales in solid (blocked) form at or beyond the given tempo. Any logical left-hand fingering is acceptable. The printed left-hand fingering is given as a suggestion.

A Major in 3rds (2 octaves)

♩ = 96

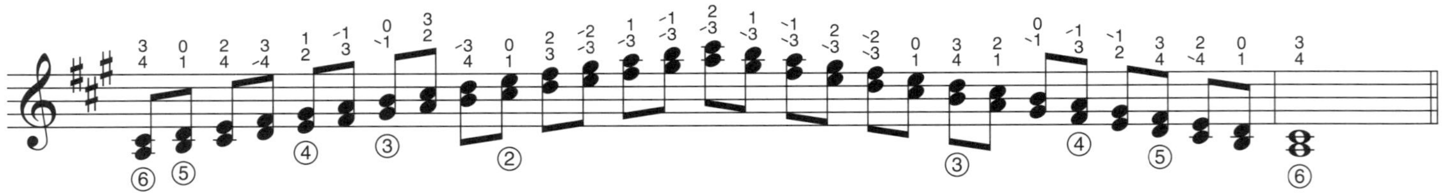

F♯ Minor Harmonic in 3rds (2 octaves)

♩ = 96

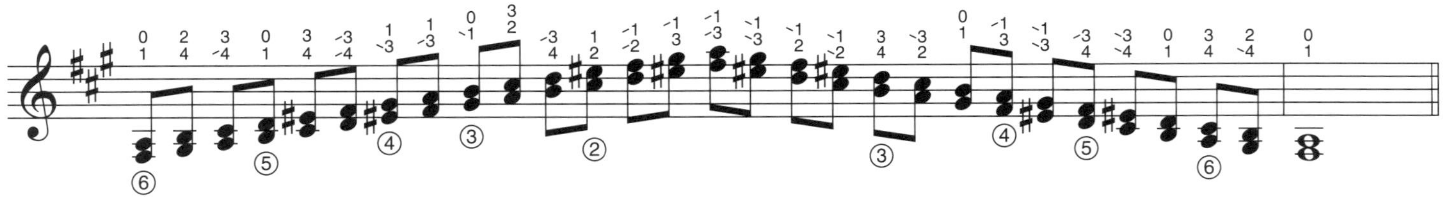

A Major in 6ths (2 octaves)

♩ = 96

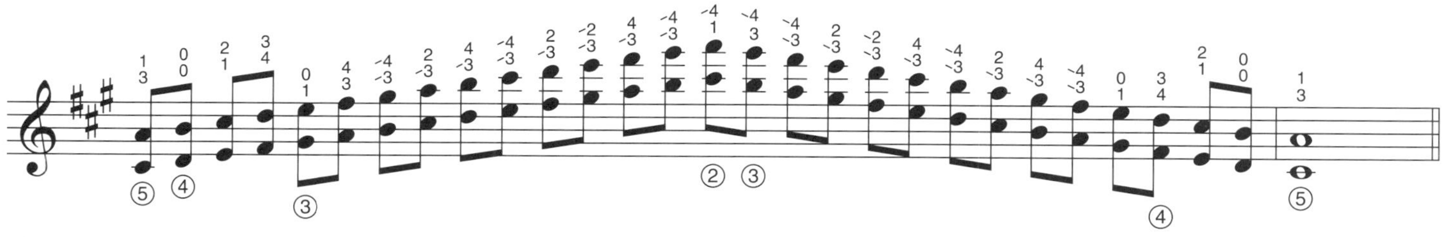

F♯ Minor Harmonic in 6ths (2 octaves)

♩ = 96

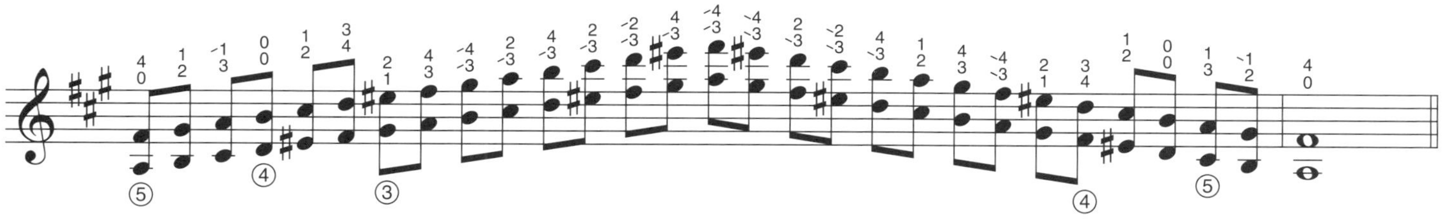

Arpeggio Patterns

Play the following arpeggio patterns at or beyond the given tempo. Use the given fingering and observe the repeat signs.

1. *p–i–m–i–a–i* alternation pattern

♩ = 72

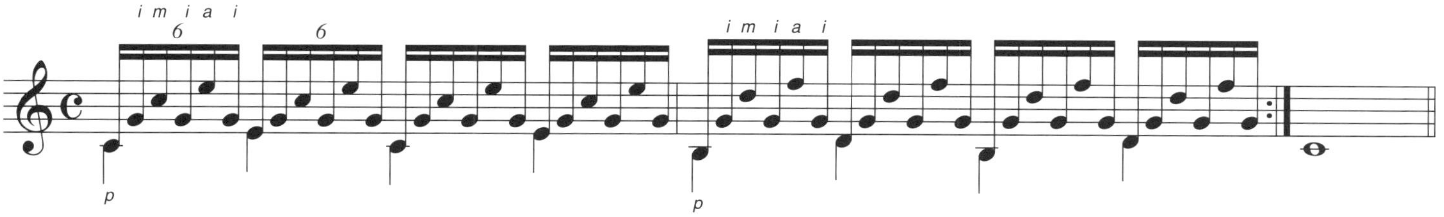

2. *p–i–a–i–m–i* alternation pattern

♩ = 72

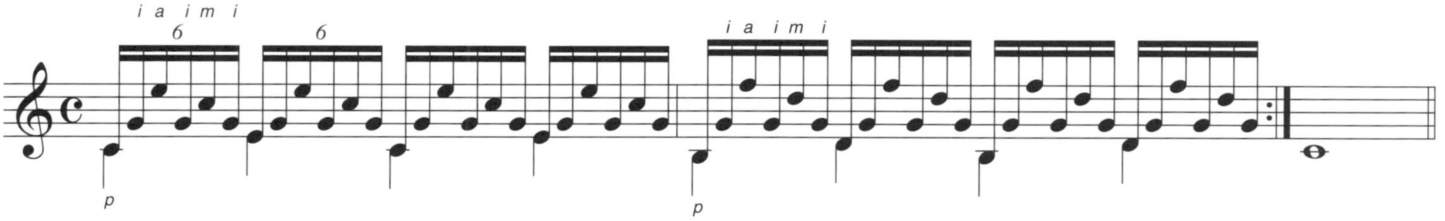

3. *p–i–m* crossing pattern

♩ = 144

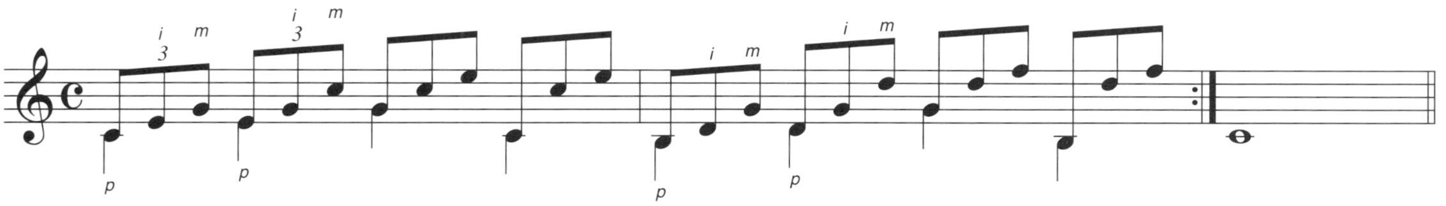

4. *m–i–p* crossing pattern

♩ = 144

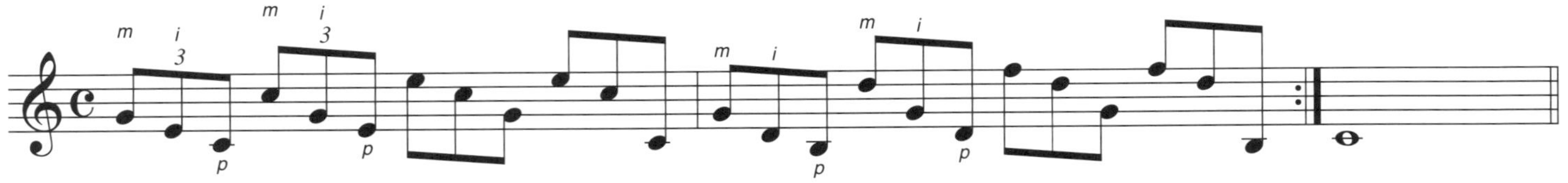

5. *p–m–i* crossing pattern

♩ = 144

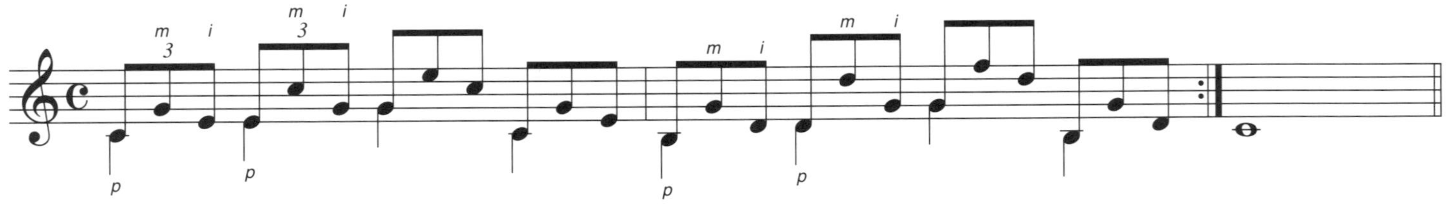

6. low–high pattern

♩ = 100

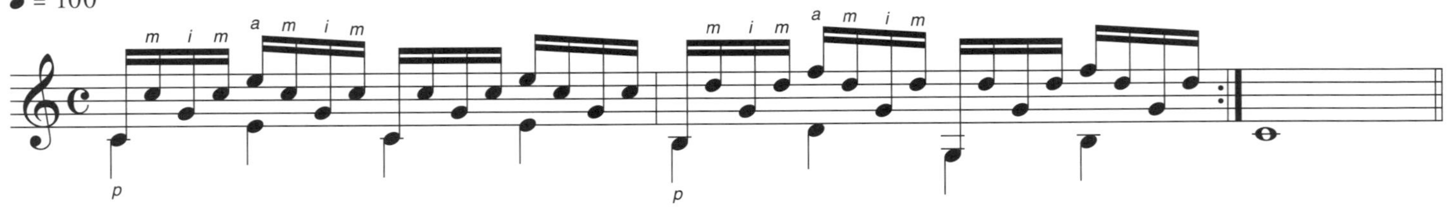

7. descending and ascending pattern

♩ = 100

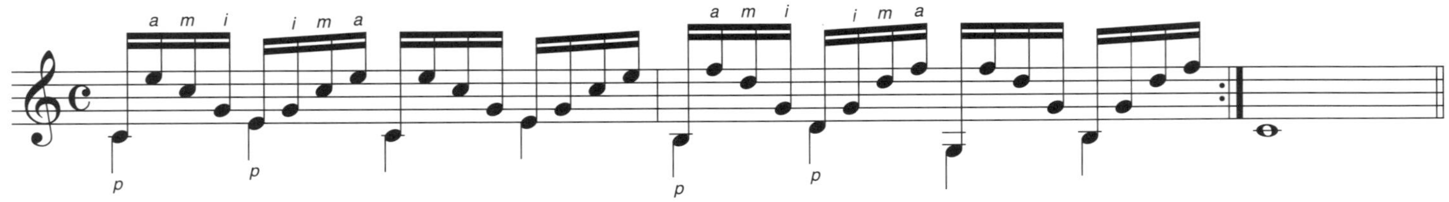

8. two-phase pattern

♩ = 100

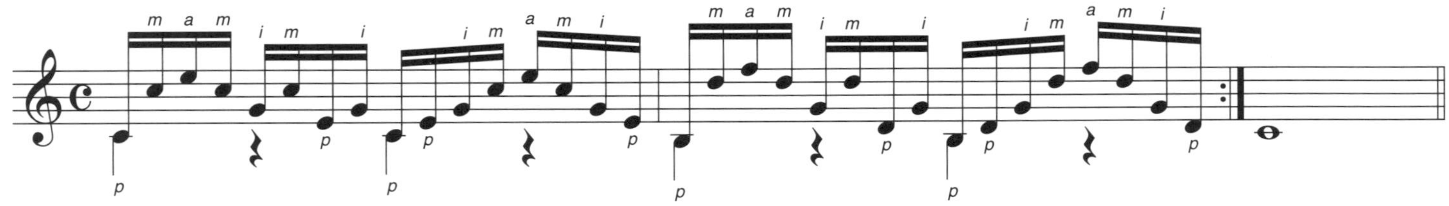

9. shifting *p–i–m–a* pattern

♩ = 108

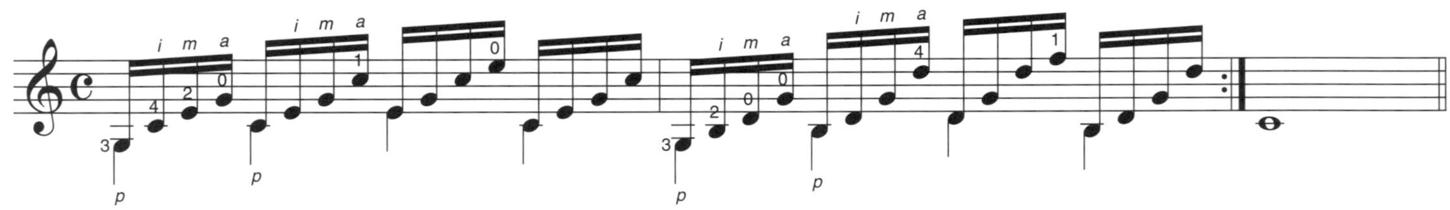

10. shifting *a–m–i–p* pattern

♩ = 108

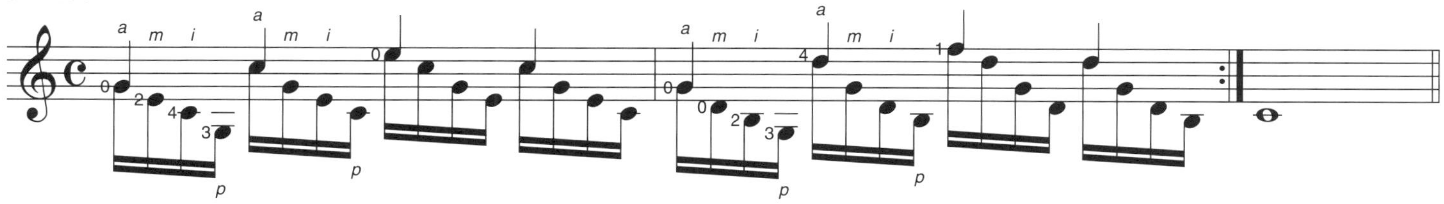

11. shifting *p–m–i–p* pattern

♩ = 92

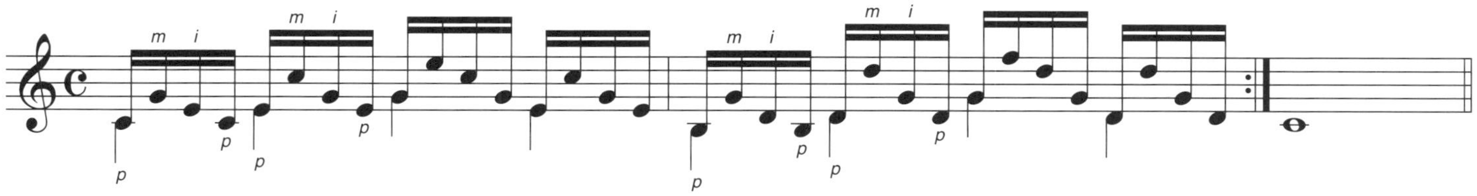

12. ascending triple-*p* pattern

♩ = 54

Level 10/ARCT

Tempos

The scales and arpeggio patterns in Level 10 are also those required for the Teacher's ARCT examination. Tempos provided are for Level 10 only. ARCT candidates should consult the *Guitar Syllabus, 2011 Edition* for tempos for that level.

Diatonic and Chromatic Scales

Play the following scales, in both rest stroke and free stroke, at or beyond the tempo given in the chart. Any logical left-hand fingering is acceptable. Finish each diatonic scale with the given cadence. Play each scale with the note values and the right-hand fingering listed in the chart. See "Accent and Fingering Patterns" on p. 6.

	Keys	Tempo	Note Values	RH Fingering
Diatonic	G, D, B, F, B♭ major E, B, G♯, D, G minor (harmonic and melodic)	♩ = 116	𝅘𝅥𝅮𝅘𝅥𝅮𝅘𝅥𝅮 (3) and 𝅘𝅥𝅯𝅘𝅥𝅯𝅘𝅥𝅯𝅘𝅥𝅯	*im* or *mi* *ia* or *ai*
Chromatic	Beginning on B	♩ = 100		*ma* or *am*

Diatonic Scales

G Major (3 octaves)

E Minor Harmonic (3 octaves)

E Minor Melodic (3 octaves)

D Major (2 octaves)

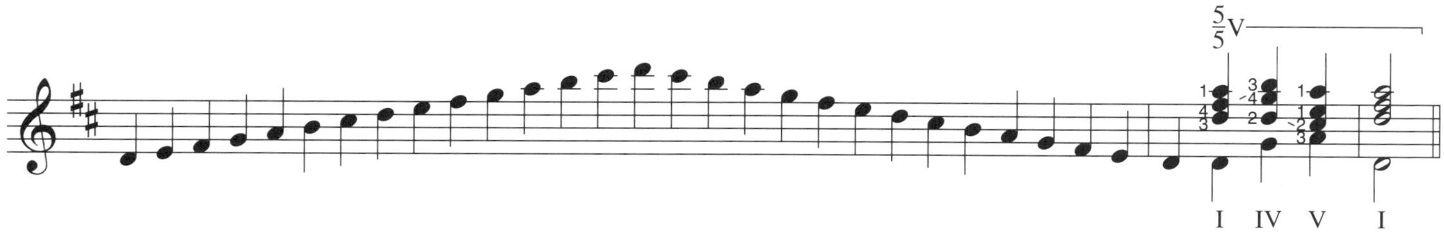

B Minor Harmonic (3 octaves)

B Minor Melodic (3 octaves)

B Major (3 octaves)

G♯ Minor Harmonic (3 octaves)

G♯ Minor Melodic (3 octaves)

F Major (2 octaves)

D Minor Harmonic (2 octaves)

D Minor Melodic (2 octaves)

B♭ Major (3 octaves)

G Minor Harmonic (3 octaves)

G Minor Melodic (3 octaves)

Chromatic Scale

Beginning on B (3 octaves)

Tremolando Scales

Play the two-octave, single-note diatonic scales illustrated above in tremolando, with both rest stroke and free stroke, at or beyond the tempo given in the chart. Any logical left-hand fingering is acceptable. Finish each scale with the given cadence. Play each scale with the note values and the right-hand fingering listed in the chart. See "Accent and Fingering Patterns" on p. 5.

Keys	Tempo	Note Values	RH Fingering
D, F, major D minor (harmonic and melodic)	♩ = 120 ♩ = 108	♪♪♪ (3) and ♬♬	*im* or *mi* *ia* or *ai* *ma* or *am*

Slur Scales

Play the following scales at or beyond the given tempo. Any logical left-hand fingering is acceptable. The printed left-hand fingering is given as a suggestion.

C Major, compound triplets (2 octaves)

♩ = 144

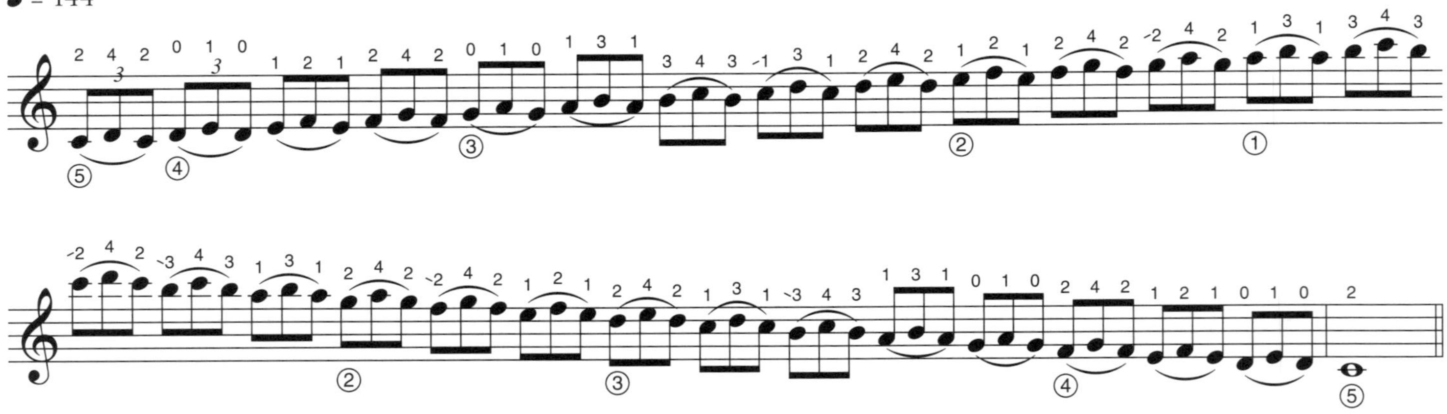

F Major, compound triplets (2 octaves)

♩ = 144

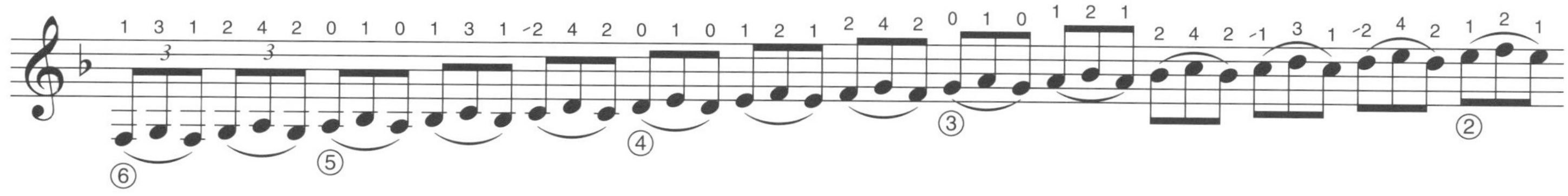

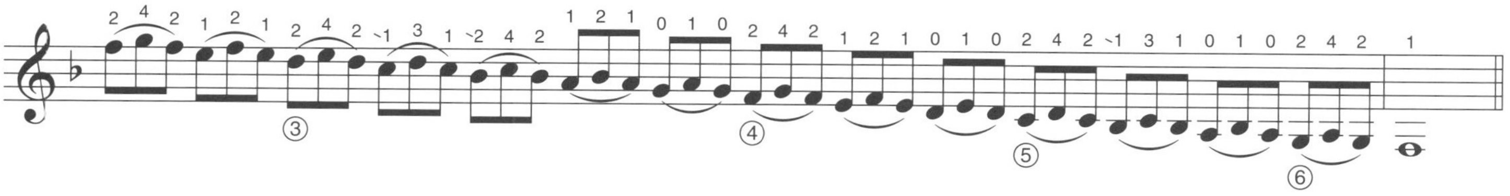

Scales in 3rds and 6ths

Play the following scales in solid (blocked) form at or beyond the given tempo. Any logical left-hand fingering is acceptable. The printed left-hand fingering is given as a suggestion.

D Major in 3rds (2 octaves)

♩ = 104

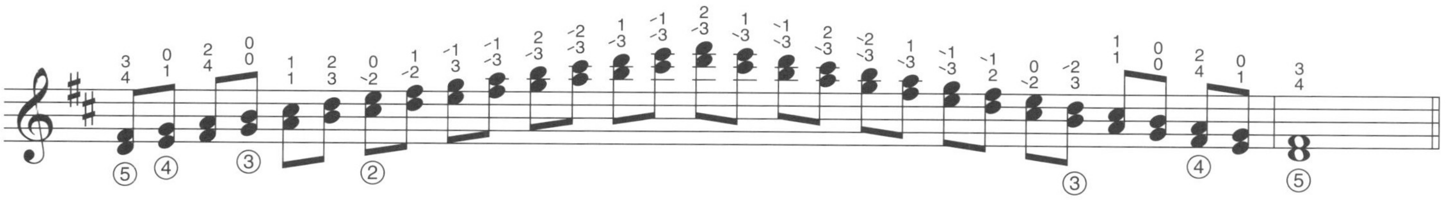

B Minor Harmonic in 3rds (2 octaves)

♩ = 104

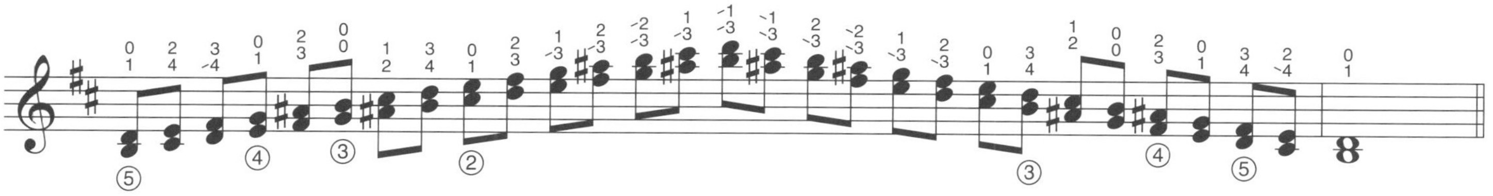

D Major in 6ths (2 octaves)

♩ = 104

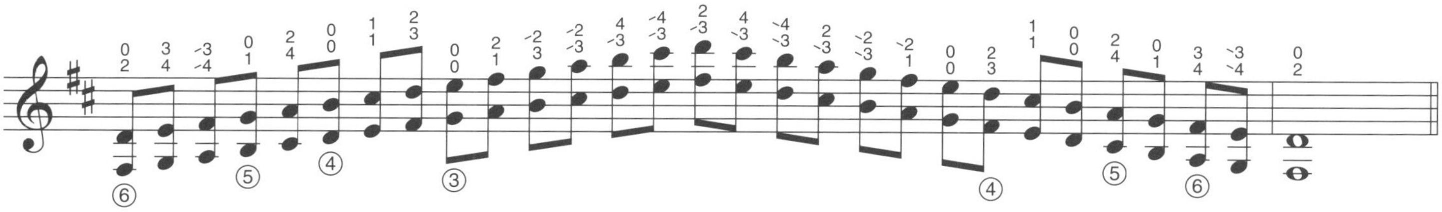

B Minor Harmonic in 6ths (2 octaves)

♩ = 104

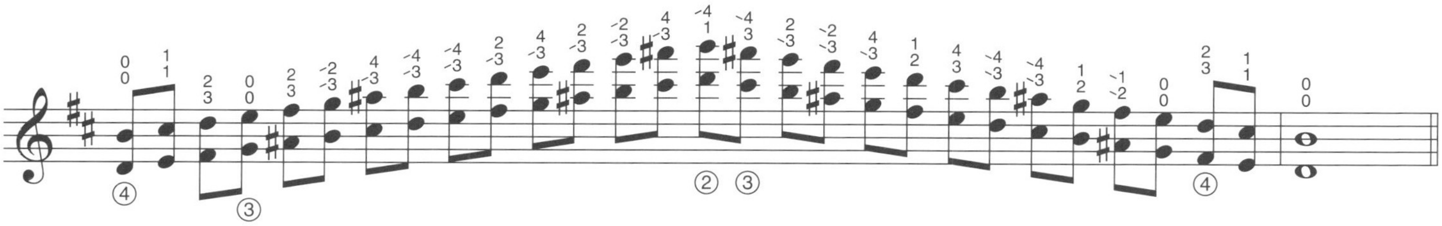

Arpeggio Patterns

Play the following arpeggio patterns at or beyond the given tempo. Use the given fingering and observe the repeat signs.

1. low–high pattern

♩ = 108

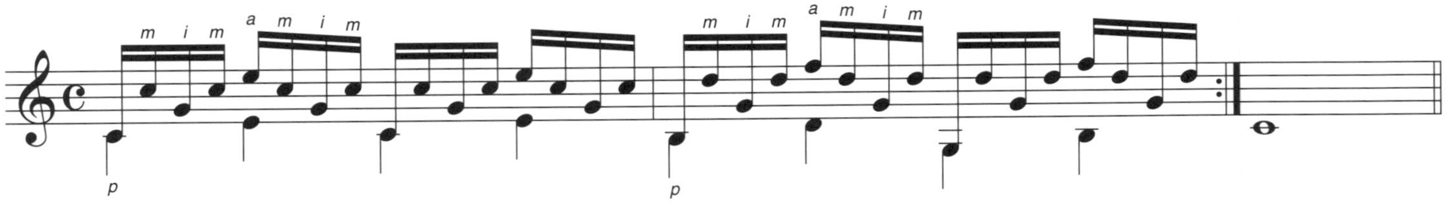

2. descending and ascending pattern

♩ = 108

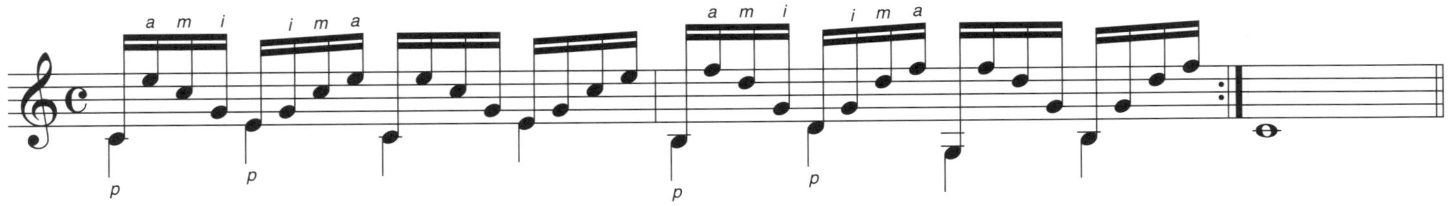

3. two-phase pattern

♩ = 108

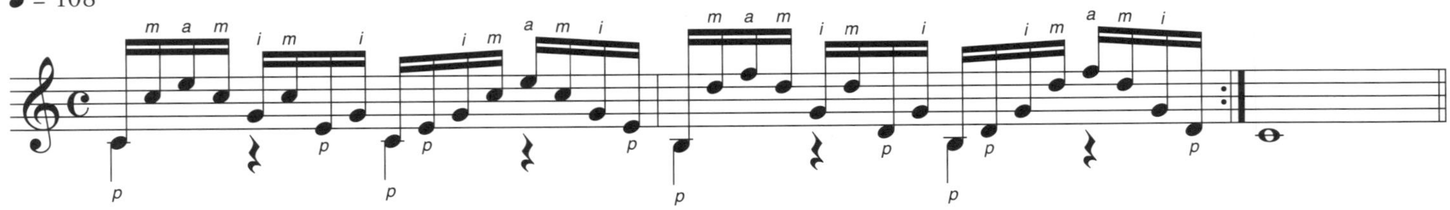

4. shifting *p–i–m–a* pattern

♩ = 116

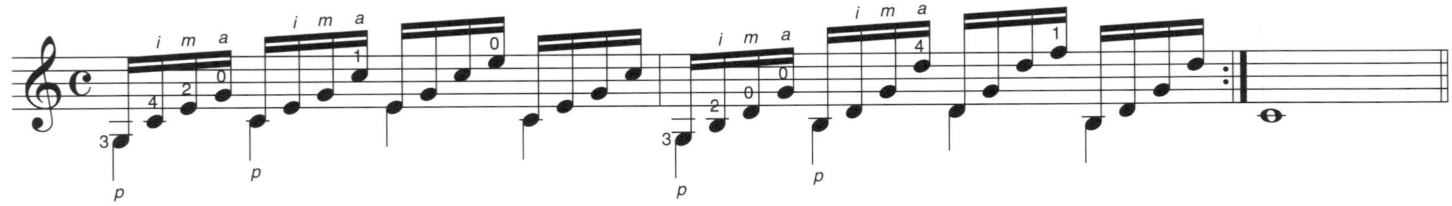

5. shifting *a–m–i–p* pattern

♩ = 116

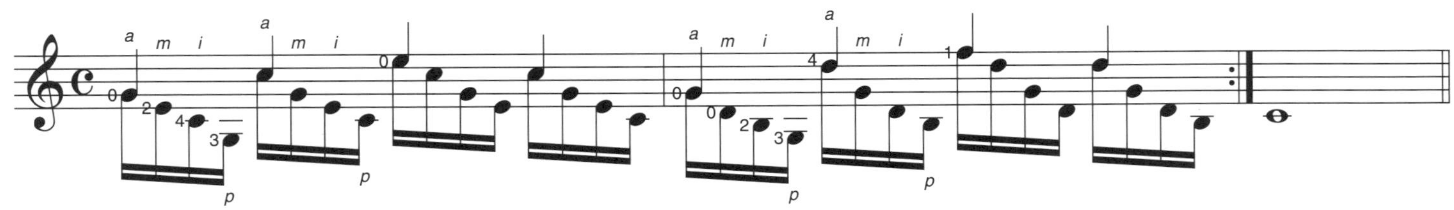

6. shifting *p–m–i–p* pattern

♩ = 100

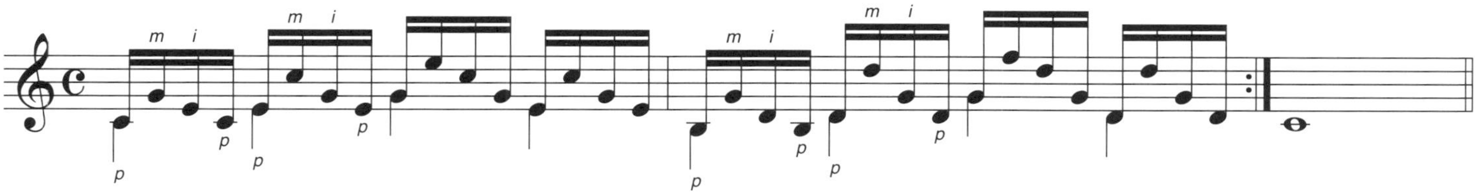

7. ascending triple-*p* pattern

♩ = 56

8. string-crossing alternation pattern

♩ = 104

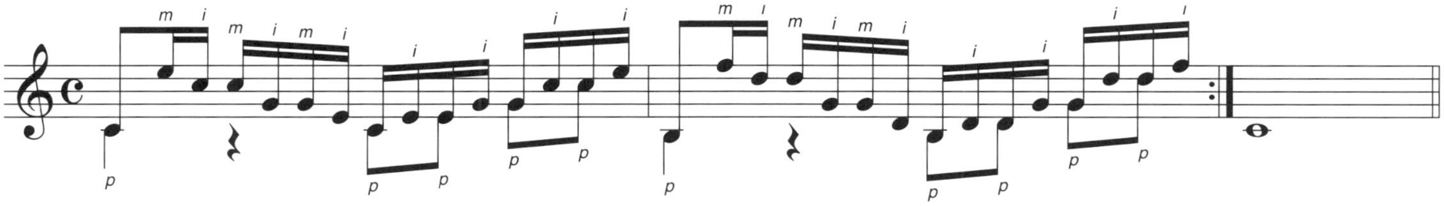

9. *p–i–m–i* crossing pattern

♩ = 104

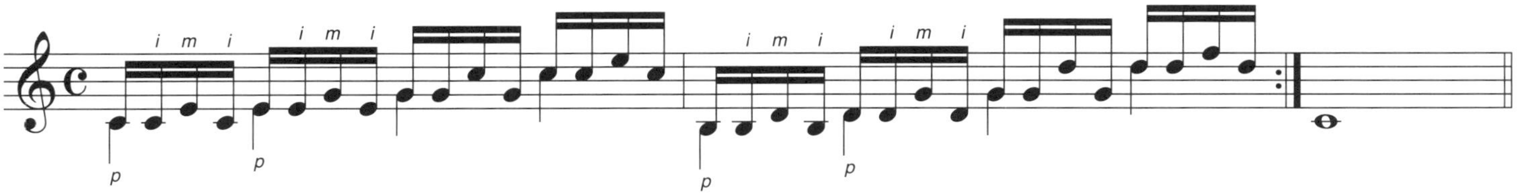

10. two-against-one alternation pattern

♩ = 108

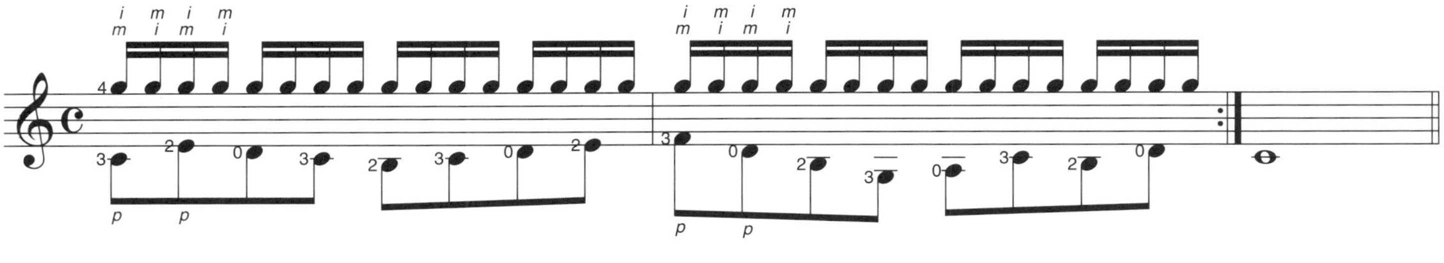

11. chord-plus-ascending-arpeggio pattern

♩ = 58

12. chord-plus-descending-arpeggio pattern

♩ = 58

Part 2: Technique Supplement

Right-hand Fingering

Diatonic, Chromatic, and Tremolando Scales

Groups of two	Groups of three	Groups of four		
i m i m	a m i a m i	a m i m	a i m i	m a i a
m i m i	m i a m i a	m i m a	m i a i	a i a m
m a m a	i a m i a m	i m a m	i m i a	i a m a
a m a m	i m a i m a	m a m i	i a i m	a m a i
i a i a	m a i m a i			
a i a i	a i m a i m			

Groups of five	Groups of six		Thumb–finger groups	
a i m i m	a i m i m i	m i a i a i	p i p i	p m p m
a m i m i	a m i m i m	m a i a i a	i p i p	m p m p
i m a m a	a m i a m i	m a i m a i	p m i	p m a
m i a i a	i m a m a m		p i m	p a m
m a i a i	i a m a m a		p a m i	p a i m
	i m a i m a		p i m a	p i a m
			p m i a	p m a i

NOTE: Groups may be linked together in various combinations, for example:

a m i m i m i m a m a m
(>) (>)

Scales in 3rds and 6ths

Scales in 3rds		Scales in 6ths
i m i m p p p p	m m i i	i m i m p p p p
m a m a p p p p	a a m m	a a a a i i i i
a m a m p i p i	m a i i	m a m a p p p p
i a i a p m p m	a a i m	m a m a p i p i

for example:

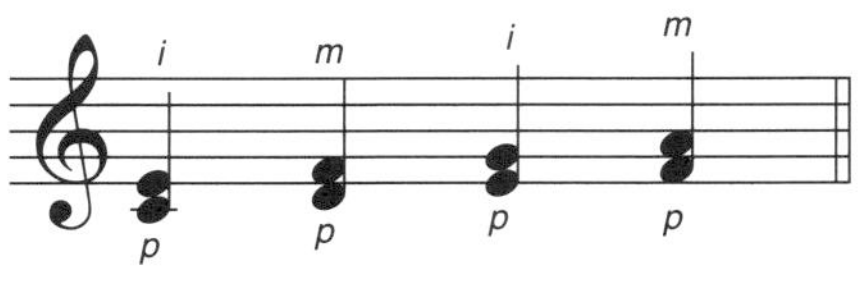

for example:

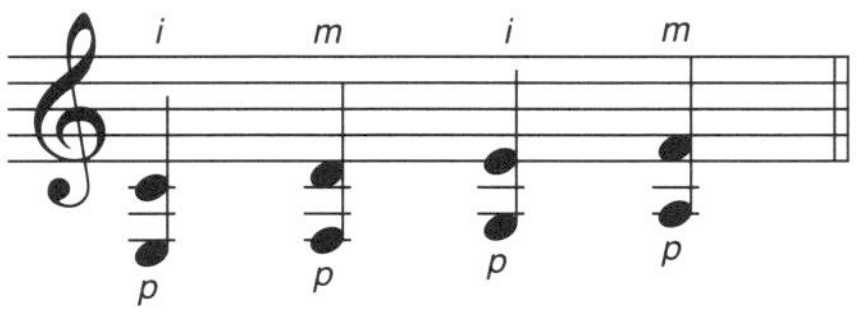

Tremolando Scales

The following example of tremolando scales in C major suggests some rhythmic variations. For fingering, see "Right-Hand Fingering" on p. 67.

Accentuations and Rhythms

Diatonic Single-note Scales

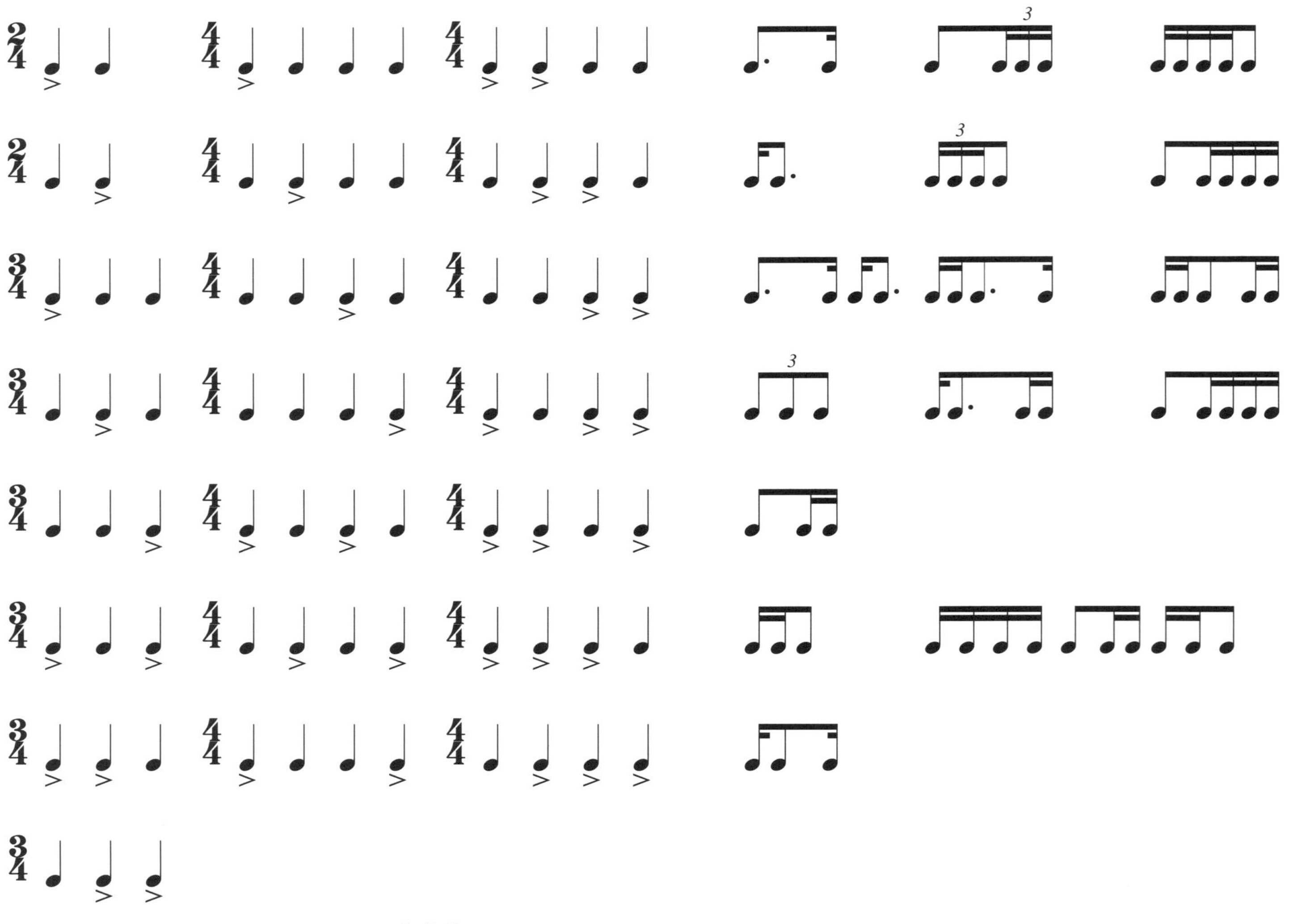

Similar accentuations may be found in $\frac{5}{4}$, $\frac{6}{4}$, $\frac{7}{4}$, and other time signatures.

Broken Forms

Scales in 3rds

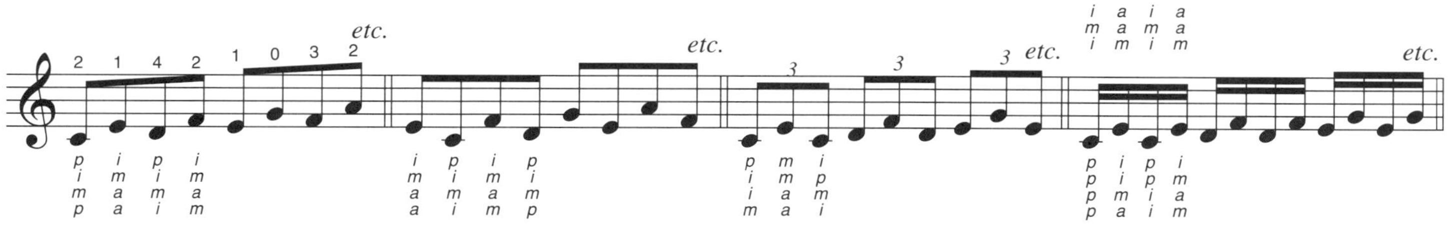

Scales in 6ths

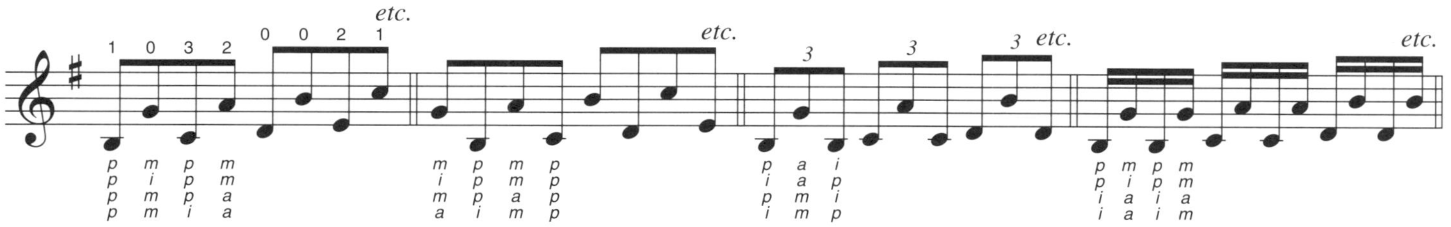

Chromatic Scales

One-octave Forms

Form 1

Form 2

Form 3

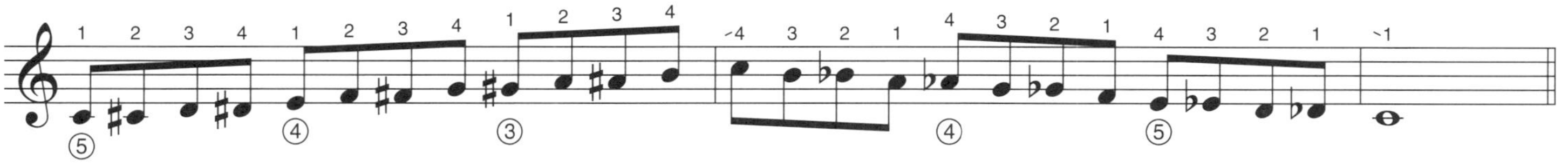

Form 4

One-octave Forms (cont'd)

One-octave forms may be combined to create longer scales.

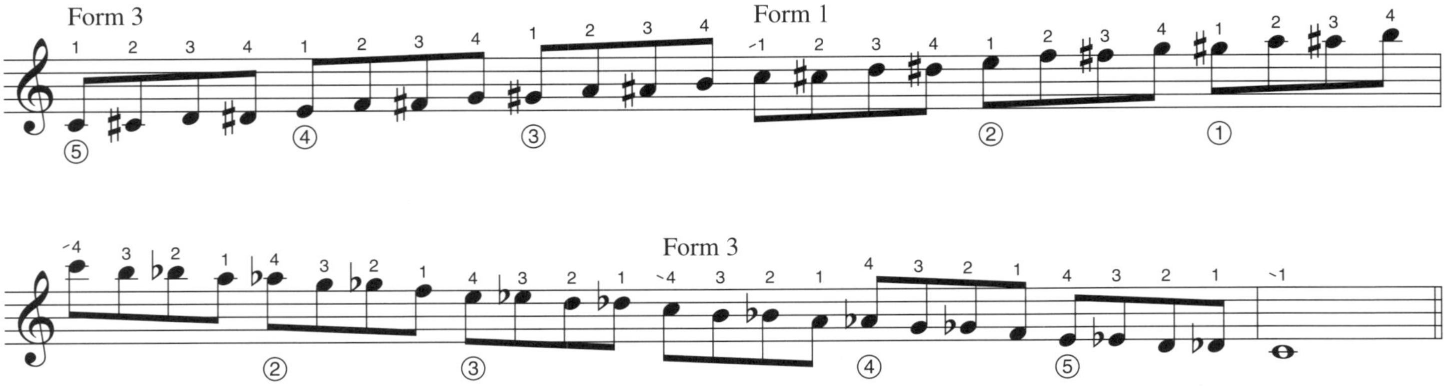

Single-string Chromatic Scale

This scale pattern may be played on any string.

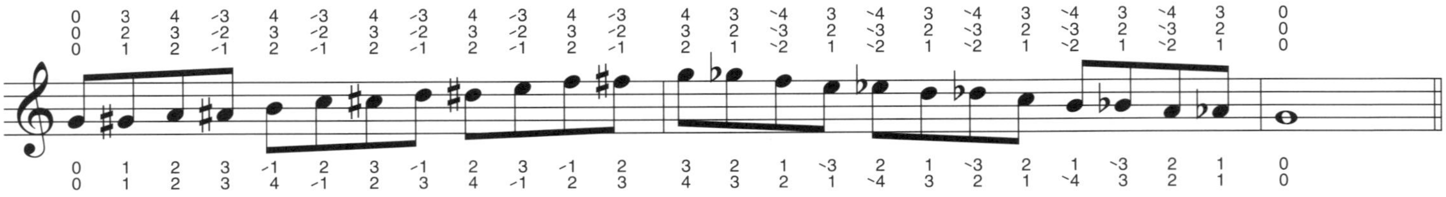

Chromatic Octaves

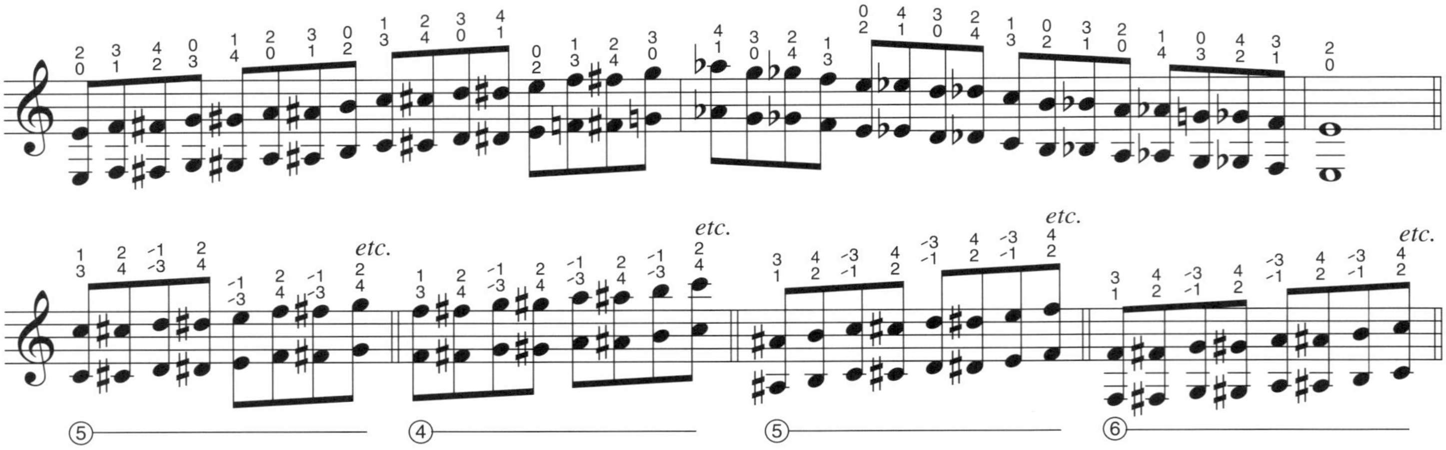

Slur Scales

Slur scale formulas may be extended to create trill exercises.

Slur scale formulas may be played without slurs as coordination studies.

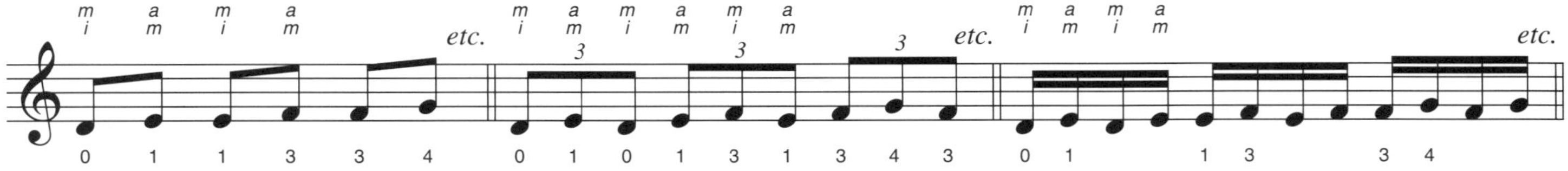

Slur scale formulas may be played partially slurred as coordination exercises.

Slur scales may be played in double-dotted rhythms as *appoggiatura* and *acciaccatura* exercises.

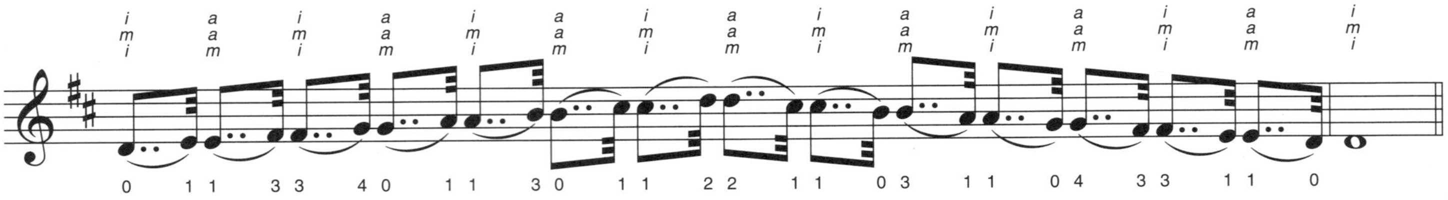

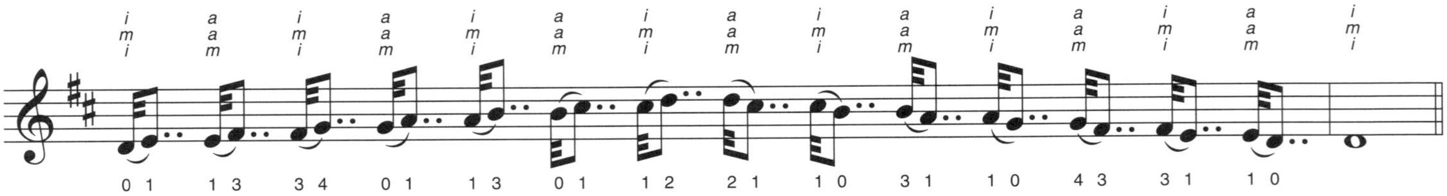

Chromatic octaves may be played with slurs.

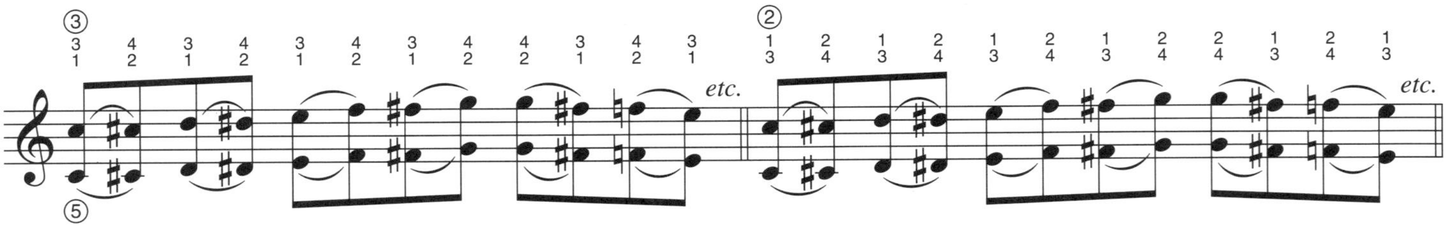

Slurs may be added to regular scale formulas as follows:

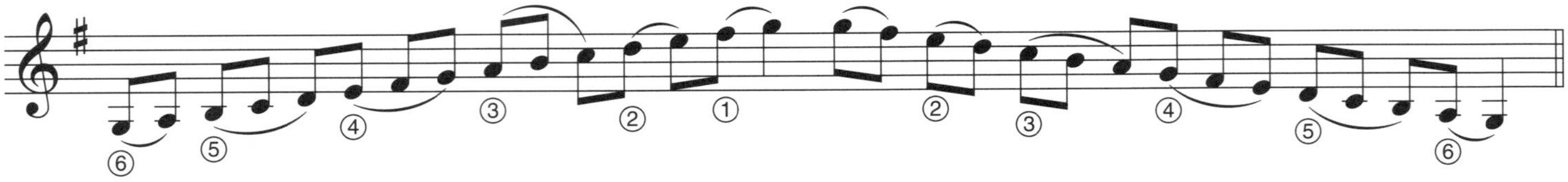

Shifting of Scale Forms

Any scale form that contains no open strings can be shifted to a higher or lower fret, thereby transposing the scale to a new key. For example, the two-octave C major scale in Level 4 (p. 19) can be shifted up to start in third position to produce a D♭ major scale. This two-octave scale form can be further transposed through D and E♭ major by starting in the fourth and fifth positions respectively. Similar transpositions are possible with the following scales:

- the two-octave F♯ major scale in Level 4 (p. 19)
- the two-octave B minor harmonic and melodic scales in Level 5 (p. 25)
- the two-octave F minor harmonic and melodic scales in Level 5 (p. 25)
- the three-octave G major scale in Level 7 (p. 35)
- the three-octave F minor harmonic and melodic scales in Level 8 (p. 45)

Naming the notes while playing the transposed scales is an effective way of becoming familiar with the different keys and acquiring fluency on the fretboard.